THE SCORE OF A LIFETIME

25 Years Talking Chicago Sports

Terry Boers

TRIUMPH
BOOKS

This book is available in quantity at special discounts for your group or organization. For further information, contact:

Triumph Books LLC
814 North Franklin Street
Chicago, Illinois 60610
(312) 337-0747
www.triumphbooks.com

Printed in U.S.A.
ISBN: 978-1-62937-575-5

Design by Patricia Frey
Photos courtesy of the author unless otherwise indicated.

To my wife, Carolyn, my guiding light for 46 years, my sons, John, Joe, Cary, and Chris, who have made me enormously proud, and my grandchildren, Tyler, Ellie, Josh, Connor, and Delaney, who remind me each and every day how beautiful life can be.

Contents

Prologue

I've always maintained that I'm one of the least interesting people in the world to interview on just about any subject.

And I say that with absolutely no hint of false modesty.

To wit: I've never been molested by a family member, a priest, a deacon, a right reverend, a wrong reverend, an elder, a monsignor, a mon-junior, a Cardinal, a Dodger, a Met, a junior-league hockey coach, a senior-league hockey coach, a gymnastics coach, Bela Karoyli, Bela Lugosi, Bella Abzug, a swimming coach, anyone with swimmer's ear, somebody else's icky uncle, Uncle Fester, Uncle Remus, Uncle Tonoose, Aunt Irma, Aunt Farm, Aunt She Sweet, Cousin Itt, anybody's distant cousin, or anyone's slightly closer cousin.

And not a single teacher I ever had in 16 years of school propositioned me, unless you count an occasional meeting where one of them would ask why I seemed so hellbent on being an idiot. 'Twas nature, not nurture.

I did have a guy at the long gone Lincoln movie theater in Chicago Heights put his hand on my knee once when I was about 8 or 9, but nothing ever came of our brief relationship. Besides, I think he might have been drunk and he could have been the usher.

I know one of my favorite college professors at Northern Illinois University would spend literally hours behind closed doors counseling nubile coeds who'd been struggling to keep their grades up. I was told he never struggled to keep his, uh…grades…up.

So no, I don't have any twisted tales of sexual depravity to share, although I understand that claiming to have been molested has become a cottage industry for some.

And no, sadly I've never sought treatment for sexual addiction, either. Nor have I ever had to sit down and tell my wife every detail of the 121 women I slept with while I was on the PGA Tour, and I've never been the subject of a song written by a certain country singer who turns every one of the guys who jilted her into songs that sound exactly the same.

I've also never been in Betty Ford or her clinic. I've never been in rehab for alcoholism or abused any illegal drugs or any prescription pain medication. I leave that to a much fatter oxymoron who's going to own a piece of an NFL team about the same time that Dallas Cowboys owner Jerry Jones admits he's had more work done on his face than Kenny Rogers.

I've never had a session with a therapist, never been ordered to anger management, never needed couples counseling, or sought anything in the way of marital aid, although I've run across plenty of dildos in my time.

So why should you keep reading?

Because I believe the journey has been pretty damn interesting. I hope you might agree.

chapter 1

Steger, USA

The late, great writer Pat Conroy knew how to paint a picture when it came to describing his hometown.

Not that he was the first to wax poetic about historic Charleston, South Carolina, as he did in his novel *South of Broad*. But who wouldn't want to grow up in a town filled with homes and buildings of classic architecture and a unique Southern charm populated by families whose centuries' old tales could be traced back to the days long before the Civil War.

From the stately elms to the other magnificent flora to the smell of the oh-so-green, green grass of home, Charleston seems like a sparkling gem, a place where you'd be proud to raise a family, a place you're almost expected to brag about to complete strangers, even if they don't give a damn.

But even as I read Conroy's remarkably descriptive work, I couldn't help but think that while Charleston may gleam, it's still located in a state where the fight to remove the Confederate flag from in front of the statehouse dragged on and on and on as each side dug in their heels.

So who really needs it?

And then there's the brilliant James Lee Burke, whose crime novels set in New Orleans and its environs have been on my must-read list for years and years. I'm reasonably sure he wasn't the first guy to write about N'awlins either, but I'm telling you he's the best. Just read one of his Dave Robicheaux novels and tell me I'm wrong. The guy is an absolute genius, a true American treasure who knows every nook, every cranny of the city and describes them with grace and elegant prose.

Even at that, I've never found New Orleans to be all that much fun after my first couple of visits. The food is great, but Bourbon Street is a grungy, filthy hellhole that attracts too many drunken imbeciles who don't know when to say when.

Again, who needs it?

Certainly not me.

I've got Steger, Illinois.

IT STILL SURPRISES me more than 65 years after the fact that so many people in the Chicago area still have no idea where Steger is. Jesus, it was founded in 1896. I've more or less given up telling people that's where I was raised because the minute you tell them you get back the look that suggests they don't know what hell you're talking about.

But then, I get that look on a wide variety of topics.

And even if you go to the trouble of saying it's about 40 miles due south of Chicago, they still look at you as if they don't know what south is.

Not that it's surprising.

I learned a long time ago that people don't give a shit about much of anything south of Chicago.

The house
I grew up
in at 3233
Sangamon St.
in Steger.

If you say you're from Highland Park or Deerfield or Winnetka or Lake Forest or any of the hoity-toity suburbs to the north, there's an immediate recognition.

Say you're from Hazel Crest or South Chicago Heights or Park Forest or Crete and you're generally considered to be white trash to some degree, depending on how many jacked-up cars can be found in your front lawn at any one time.

But I didn't know any of that when I was growing up. If I had, I no doubt would have told them to go fuck themselves. I've never cared much for people whose apparent mission in life is to put on airs in the mistaken belief they're somehow better than you because of an address.

So allow me to tell you about Steger.

As I grew up an only child in the '50s and '60s, we had two drugstores kitty corner from one another, a Kresge's dime store, a laundromat, a liquor store, a corner tap, a couple of barbershops,

11

With my cousin,
Joy Kubancek,
in 1956.

Behind the wheel
as a toddler in
the early '50s.

an American Legion, a gas station, a shoe store, a paper store, a
Dari-Whip, and a bowling alley.

I might be missing a few things, but you get the picture.

So yes, the term *small town America* certainly fits here.

I don't remember if the one restaurant we had was always
there, but I never remember eating at it. I'm pretty sure I wasn't
missing anything.

And yes, there was an attached fire station and police station notable for a couple of reasons. First and foremost, the tiny cop house actually got plenty of attention because a prisoner perished in a fire, no mean trick since the fire equipment was within 5 feet.

I remember walking up to take a look at the damage when I was around 10 or so and not thinking much of it.

Today, I'd be thinking *what kind of incredible numb nuts allows this to happen?*

I would get the answer to that question a few years later when I would have my own dealings with Steger's finest, but I'll save that for now.

About the only other negative incident came when I was accused of shoplifting from the Kresge's. I recall that one of the managers, at least I think he was, came running out after me on 34th St., claiming that I had swiped some rubber bands.

Rubber-fucking bands. This jerkoff chased me because he thought I'd taken rubber bands? Cock spank.

I allowed him to frisk me. I can't help but thinking now that's all he really wanted to do in the first place. He found no stolen goods, but still told me I was banned from ever coming in the store again.

I'm not even sure that should qualify as punishment.

The protocol these days would probably be to call the parents, but no call was ever made, nor do I recall ever telling my mom and dad that this had happened. I like that policy.

I have no idea whatever became of this guy, but I'm thinking that his frisk was more than a little too vigorous. It's possible I'm just imagining that after all these years, but I have a feeling I wasn't the last kid he checked.

Why none of this made sense is that my grandmother worked at the paper store across the street and I could go and get anything that I wanted, which usually meant candy.

I didn't realize it at the time—probably because I was too busy shoving Hershey bars down my yap—that my grandmother was one of the sweetest people alive.

I thought about her when I became a grandfather for the first time, which just happens to be one of the most extraordinary experiences of anyone's life. The birth of Tyler Joseph Boers on St. Patrick's Day in 2003 forever enriched my life to a point I would have never imagined, just as did the other four grandchildren who were to follow.

Anyway, the fact my grandmother would later marry the Steger equivalent of Mayberry's Otis Campbell no doubt created a stir I didn't know about.

This guy was a drunk's drunk, someone who according to many spent plenty of nights in his car sleeping one off. And, I have to assume, at times he probably drove it with the proverbial snootful.

Still, while I would later learn that he could be a mean drunk upon occasion, he always was good to me, which at the time meant he showed no inclination to frisk me.

The only other hazard around town that immediately comes to mind was from a guy everyone called Titchy.

I can't remember his real name because there's a chance I never really knew it. I also understand that in today's world you'd never get away with poking fun at someone's disability. Sorry, but Titchy it is. And no, I never found out what ailed him. But I never really asked.

Here's what I knew from an early age: people were deathly afraid of him behind the wheel of his beat-up blue Chevrolet.

I recall standing on the north side of 34th Street and watching this guy come barreling down the old main drag. More than once you'd see him crossing the center line and getting into the other lane, or perhaps he'd be veering towards the curb. He was a pinball wizard.

A victim of apparent spasmodic reactions in both of his arms and apparently his head, his driving was unpredictable and dangerous. It was kind of like you had access to a puppet show at 50 miles per hour. And while some in town insisted that he had a driver's license, no one could figure out how he passed the test.

Again, I don't know what became of him, although I suppose stunt driving might have been his true calling. Someone should have called Joie Chitwood. You might have to look that one up.

At any rate, I hope you're getting the picture here. I don't think Steger was all that different from many of the small towns in America in the mid-1950s. The one thing I can assure you is that we didn't hear from countless social workers, psychologists, and other experts about the dos and don'ts of raising children.

I kind of think that's a good thing. I'm not opposed to getting help for those who need it, but I would later learn that some plain old common sense could do wonders.

Besides, who's to really say if one generation is better than the next?

I was a product of parents who were part of what was to become known as The Greatest Generation. Pretty hard to beat that.

Do you want to argue about the success of the Baby Boomers vs. the Millennials? Have fun. If people today are convinced they're raising the best and the brightest kids in the history of mankind because of the all the parental advice out there, good for them. Even if they're impossibly full of shit.

We always wanted our four kids to learn to think for themselves, to have a strong moral compass, and to understand that life isn't always going to be a smooth ride, that how you cope with the difficult times says much more about you as a person than how you act when things are going well.

But I'm not about to lecture anyone on good parenting. You can be a terrific parent and wind up with a kid (or kids) who are impossible shitheads.

I just wish that so many of the fumble-fucks out there didn't have so many idiot children. I also wish that Titchy had been a safer, more considerate driver. Today, he'd look just like one of those idiots texting while they're driving.

chapter 2

Radio Calling

I'm not positive when I first heard there were plans to start an all-sports radio station in Chicago, although there had been a few whispers here and there in the first couple months of 1991.

Did it pique my interest? Sure did. But I don't recall seeking any detailed information. About the only thing I knew for sure was that Dan McNeil was supposedly involved. While the producer for Chet Coppock's show, McNeil and I had worked a few shows together when Coppock was on vacation. I'd been a semi-regular with Chet when I was covering the Bulls and later when I wrote a column.

Thing is, there wasn't much feedback on what we'd done. But then I didn't expect much considering Coppock's audience didn't come within light years of matching his ego.

Later in the decade, 1988 to be more precise, I worked for more than three years on The Sportswriters Sunday afternoons on WGN radio, which was the city's AM monster at the time. But I didn't think that spending a few hours with my old running buddy Dave van Dyck of the *Sun-Times*, the colorful Bill Jauss of the *Chicago Tribune*, and legendary host Ben Bentley had a damn thing to do with 'GN being king of the hill. But it was a thing, especially with Bentley, who, even if it was the height of Bears season or the coldest day of the year, always fretted during breaks, wondering when we were going to get to the Cubs.

As for the earlier shows I'd done with Danny, they might have been good, they might have been have been bad or, perhaps, just okay. I never knew and never spent a moment worrying about it. We always had fun. That's what mattered most.

And at no point during any of this did I suspect, nor particularly crave, making a career change to radio. There just wasn't the opportunity to be had and I didn't even pretend to know much about the medium, unless you count being able to turn one on and off as a strength.

The one thing I could relate to was a decided lack of feedback from print or radio. Not that I ever expected to hear much in the way of hosannas or hate-yous in the snail mail era. That's what you call being conditioned to seldom hear a discouraging word. Or any other word for that matter.

When you'd worked at newspapers as long as I had, you got pretty used to the idea that only upon the rarest occasion does anyone in a position of power ever even say "nice job." The most you'd ever receive was an occasional nod and perhaps one of the paper's big shots actually recognized you in the hallway. Not likely, but it could happen.

And the lot of a desk guy is even worse if attention is what you seek.

For example, the first time I ran into the legendary *Sun-Times* columnist Irv Kupcinet at the paper was in the bathroom.

Old Irv barely grunted at me in 1980, which was soon after I started on the night sports desk. I walked away with the distinct impression Kup was kind of expecting me to hand him a paper towel.

As for Mike Royko, no doubt the greatest columnist in the history of the city, he walked right by me many, many times without saying a word. Good thing he wasn't moving fast enough to give him windburn.

It had to be just before I left the desk to take the Bulls beat that I was right behind Royko as he was getting a cup of coffee at a machine in the newsroom. Before the coffee stopped pouring, Royko suddenly started to keel over backwards. I grabbed him up, thinking that he was having some kind of health issue.

After I steadied him, Royko muttered what sounded to be a thank you, took his coffee, and shuffled back to his office. I kind of think that Royko might have been sloshed that night, hardly a surprise considering his reputation.

There were a few other nights when I'd see him at the Billy Goat Tavern, sitting at the corner of the bar looking in worse shape than most coma patients.

Let's leave it at this. I absolutely loved Royko's work. He might have been a good guy. I never found out. But then what I thought didn't matter much. With apologies to horse-racing maven Dave Feldman, Royko was The One and Only King.

I WAS BACK to writing features by 1991, "retiring" from the column after the relatively new guys running the *Sun-Times* accused me of writing a column about a Bears-Dallas game in which I had purportedly used overtones throughout that the Marlboro Man—he of the well-known ad campaign at the time—was gay. I couldn't believe it. I also couldn't believe that they didn't think the Marlboro Man was gay.

Rather than continue to argue what was clearly going to be a losing cause, I stepped back and told them that I would give up the job, one which had netted me three quick writing awards, including the 1989 Peter Lisagor award. In Chicago, you can't do any better.

Truth is, the timing was perfect. My son, Joe, had just embarked on what was going to be a terrific high school athletic career, and I'd always chafed a bit at the idea of being out of town so much. This was the perfect opportunity to grab back at least some of my life.

And if that weren't enough, how about the fact that the guy I would have to answer to: The one, the only Steve Rosenbloom, who was assignment editor for Toyland, as the sports department was known. For his part, Steve denies that ever happened. It happened. I loved him then and I love him now, especially in his role as the man behind Chicago's funniest Snark Tank.

I was covering Illinois sports and writing the occasional feature piece when I received a phone call from someone by the name of Seth Mason, who asked if I'd be willing to come in for an interview involving the all-sports radio station.

Mason, as I would later learn, had helped make WXRT-FM into one of radio's gold standards, along with Diamond Broadcast owner Dan Lee, who would turn out to be one of the best people I've ever known.

Despite some rather large changes in ownership, 'XRT remains the same great station to this very day, thanks to true legends like Lin Brehmer, Terri Hemmert, and Frank E. Lee, all of whom are still around.

At the time, 'XRT was located at 4949 W. Belmont in the city. Easy enough. I was told to just go west on Belmont off the Kennedy Expressway and look for the giant radio tower on my left-hand side.

Given those directions, how many people do you think would have managed to drive right by the building and go on for a couple of miles? Only when I realized that I was way beyond Central Ave. did it occur to me that I'd screwed up. Finally I turned the car around and headed back. And you know what I saw almost immediately? The tower. Idiot.

When I got back to the rather unimpressive light brick building on my right-hand side, I noticed a car coming out of a gated parking lot on my left.

That's for me I thought, quickly pulling in before the gate closed.

Of course, I would later have to have someone come out of the radio station to let me out because while it was indeed the 'XRT lot, you needed a clicker.

So I was already off to a roaring start.

As for Mason, he was completely cordial as we visited, even though I could tell he wasn't the world's greatest sports fan. In later years it was a delight to watch the interaction between McNeil and Mason. While I assumed there was a mutual respect, there were certainly some days when they clashed in a rather loud fashion. I would come to find out that was just Danny being Danny. I'm pretty sure Seth felt the same way. Talk about a guy who could keep his cool even under barrage. That was Seth.

By the end of our conversation that day, Mason had mapped out the plan for the station, telling me that he'd already hired

Mike North, who, in Mason's words, "was going to become a big star." I had no idea who North was. I would find out soon enough.

As for me, I wasn't sure about much of anything.

There was no offer of a job that day, but I certainly liked Mason and his plan seemed to make sense in a city as crazy about sports as Chicago.

But thinking something doesn't make it true.

Sure, Chicagoans loved their sports, but if the station turned out to be a big, fat flop, what then?

I spent more time worrying about something I hadn't even been invited to than seems humanly possible, keeping in mind that WFAN in New York had become this country's first fulltime all-sports radio station in 1987 and seemed to be going great.

On the other hand, taking such a career risk with four kids and a big mortgage didn't seem to make a lot of sense, even if I'd had it with the *Sun-Times*.

I was clearly at a crossroads in my career. Yes, the column was gone, but the checks were still coming in. Did I hate my job? Probably more than I was willing to admit, although my assignments were just fine. Was I completely ready to put writing in the rearview mirror? Didn't want to, but it's a tough go when your bosses don't have your back in any business, especially newspapers.

But I wasn't completely blind to what was going on in the world.

I can recall telling anyone who'd listen that newspapers were going to be in trouble sometime not too far in the future. It had become clear to me that at a time when Americans wanted to be entertained by just about everything, newspapers weren't exactly holding up their end of the bargain.

Did that mean massive closings? Massive job layoffs? The untimely death of the newspaper business?

I wouldn't have gone that far back then. Turns out a lot of papers apparently didn't, either. And many of them are long gone by now.

Having worked at the craft for 20 years, there was never a hint of glee in my voice. I have no idea on God's green—and too often angry—earth where I would have been without the opportunities I was given.

I didn't really care for the food business—fast or otherwise—and the only other job I'd ever done was at a paint factory in Chicago Heights, where I'd worked three summers. It was there that I ran headlong into a guy who relished bullying people, especially "college boys."

And while I generally had escaped such stupidity to that point, he was insistent on being a prick. He just couldn't let a day go by without approaching me in a threatening manner, always coming up with something about me that seemed to bother him to no end.

He was probably around 5'10", a solid 190 pounds or so, right around 35 years old. He clearly took care of himself physically and came to work in blue coveralls that he somehow made look menacing. No easy trick. He had this harsh little bite to his words, making sure that nothing was left to the imagination. Do something he didn't like and I knew he would make good on his veiled threats. "I'd love to bust you up," I remember him saying to me one morning. I didn't respond.

He never carried out the threat, but he remained very much in the picture until I joined the factory's softball team. I'd never really played 12-inch fast pitch before, but it turned out to be my road to a safe harbor. Playing against other factory workers from around the Heights, the games tended to be on the rough-and-tumble side. There were plenty of tough guys around, but this element was good for me. The vast majority of them probably would have kicked my ass off the field, but on field was a different story.

I hit enough of everything to keep them happy, finally fitting in with a culture I didn't even know existed.

But I digress.

As things played out, I was going to have to make up my mind in a very short amount of time. The clock was ticking and Diamond Broadcasting had already purchased the AM 820 frequency for $650,000.

But even at that point, despite all the hand-wringing and angst, I genuinely didn't know what would happen if the offer actually came.

And the offer was to come.

chapter 3

Mom and Dad

My dad's full name was John Henry Boers. He was born May 26, 1917, and was raised on a farm just outside the bustling metropolis of Monee, Illinois, with three siblings, sisters Pearl and Della and brother Chris.

I know he was a terrific baseball player in his youth, once turning down an offer to play in the old Three-I League. He eventually enlisted in the army along with just about every other red-blooded American following the bombing of Pearl Harbor.

He fought mainly in Italy with the 34th infantry division, telling me he was there the day Italian dictator Benito Mussolini was hung upside down in the suburban square of Piazzale Loreto in Milan. While historical accounts of those days often differed, this much seems true: Mussolini had been killed near the village of Dongo on Lake Como by anti-fascist Italians, then brought to Milan where many Italians would further abuse the body after it was hung on a steel girder.

My dad said he just didn't have the stomach for that sort of thing, that he saw the body from a distance and that was good enough.

I believe I was 10 when he told me that story. And it was to be the last war story he would ever share. Like most vets, he never wanted to talk about his experiences. And the fighting in Italy had been just as bloody, just as horrific as it had been elsewhere in Europe and the Pacific.

What I have left today is the flag that was draped over his coffin after he died of a heart attack in January 1974, a box full of military medals I keep in my living room, and a couple of pictures I cherish, including one of him holding John, the only grandson he would ever know, albeit far too briefly.

I never knew my dad's dad. I do remember the trip we once took to visit him at a nursing facility in Peotone. I was probably 3 or 4 at the oldest, so the memories are hazy and, in all honesty, just about gone. For some odd reason what I most vividly recall was the overwhelming antiseptic smell that washed over you the second you walked in the place. I don't know if was liniment or some kind of spray or something else entirely, but it has stuck in my senses for all these years. And if you're of a certain age, you might remember it, too.

As for my grandfather, he was exceedingly frail, confined to a wheelchair with a red and black blanket tucked snugly on his lap.

I don't remember what he said that day, but my belief is it wasn't very much. Just like my dad, he was a man of few words, although it's possible that wasn't his fault, that the whole thing might have been too painful in every sense of the word for him.

Sadly, that visit was the only one I truly recall. There might have been a few others, but I honestly don't remember. I never knew what I was missing.

My dad fought for our country in World War II.

While I'm sure I was told that my grandpa had passed, I also don't have a single recollection of the wake or funeral. It's also possible I didn't go. It's just as possible that there never was a visitation.

Only much later would I fully comprehend just how important that one day must have been to a dying man. I will never forget how my mom and dad swelled with pride when they got their first glimpse of my first son, John, who was born on August 16, 1971.

Perhaps that's why I've always admired guys like the late Tim Russert, not only for his great interviewing skills during his years on *Meet the Press*, but also for his remarkable ability to recall enough details about his father to write an entire book about their relationship.

The first time I saw that book on the shelves I was horribly jealous and envious. I might have even cried.

As selfish as it might sound, I've always felt horribly cheated that my dad and mom, more about her in a moment, both died at the age of 56.

I so desperately wanted to share with them the turns my life would take, the good, the bad, the birth of three more kids, my professional ups and downs, and every other part of my life.

It would have been nice if they'd both lived long enough to see their sometimes idiotic, often directionless only child prove that he did have some abilities besides a penchant for getting in trouble with his questionable driving and a seeming willingness to skate through school even though my test scores always indicated I should have done much better.

But that never really occurred to me. I suppose things haven't really changed that much. There are hundreds more distractions for kids today than there ever were for me. I just couldn't wrap my head around any of it, particularly when I started at Bloom High School, where the sheer numbers were enough to overwhelm you.

MY MOM, BORN Ruth Rubottom, traced her roots back to Massachusetts and Ireland.

Her mother, Marian, who happened to be the only grandparent I ever really knew, was born a twin, but her sister had died in childbirth.

I seem to recall her telling me that she met my dad shortly after he returned from the war in 1945, but my aunt once told me it was a few years later on a blind date.

My mom in 1958.

Doesn't matter.

I do know that of the two, she was by far the most dogmatic, the most likely to tell me when I was being a fool, and the most likely to vent her frustrations verbally.

In other words, the most like me.

I promise you that if there'd been timeouts for kids back then, I probably would have spent the equivalent of about two years in limbo.

So yes, while my dad possessed the easiest going disposition of just about anyone I've ever known, my mom had the ability to see right through my bullshit.

You have to remember that back then most mothers didn't work and most didn't drive a car. It's safe to say I was her full-time project. I didn't mean to be. I just was. I can't say her lessons of life were any different than any parent would teach today, but many of the things she attempted to instill remain timeless, no matter which generation you're talking about.

I know this. The two of them made quite a team and there was no place for me to hide in our tiny, two-bedroom, one-bath house at 3233 Sangamon St.

MUCH OF WHAT was said was no doubt lost on me at the time (actually, anything with the exception of a candy bar was lost on me).

I was 11 when my dad, coming completely from out of the blue, suggested that it might be time to start earning a little money.

Here's what he wanted me do to. Go with him on Sunday mornings to Dixie Dairy in Chicago Heights, where he was employed as a mechanic. The job? Wash giant, filthy milk trucks. For every one cleaned, the reward was $3.00, which actually sounded pretty good at the time.

On that first Sunday, he presented me with a hose, a bucket of soapy water, and a long-handled brush. "Get to work," he said. "I'm not going to be here that long today."

I don't know how many people less than 30 years of age have ever even seen a milk truck, but believe me it looked as if it had escaped from the pack and rolled around in the mud for an hour.

I did the best I could, or at least so I thought. But the final product was never, ever quite done to his satisfaction.

He'd look at a truck I'd been working on for 45 minutes and ask when was I going to start on it.

Thing is, I know he was right.

The truck looked like crap, so he'd have to spend another 30 minutes of his time touching it up rather than fixing the vehicles he'd come to repair. And Sundays were supposed to be his days off.

You'd think that at least one goddamn time I'd have gotten it right during those first three months or so. I mean nobody was going to come back and inspect the trucks with a white glove to my knowledge and it certainly didn't seem a matter of life or death. I don't know if slightly dirty trucks turned people off. I don't know if company policy insisted the trucks had to gleam. All I knew is that I loved their chocolate milk.

That Sunday morning trip was to become a staple, even if I was just a tad slow on the uptake.

I can happily say that I did get better at it, but it was a painful process. Only in the last few weeks was I able to figure out that I had to make sure I got the very top of the truck to shine, no easy task considering much of the fleet had more than 125,000 miles on the odometer.

I think my dad smiled the first time one of the trucks was actually done to his satisfaction. But by the time he'd brought in another dirty one from the lot, he was back to being pretty quiet.

He might have used the term "put a little elbow grease in it" once or twice. I do know that a few years later one of my friend's dads told him to put some elbow grease in it and my friend spent two hours in his garage looking for it.

Anyway, I still think about those muck-covered monsters every so often, mostly during quiet moments.

I can't say for sure that was his way of telling me to reach a little higher. That might be a little much. Besides, even if he was a guy of few words, I think he would have said it.

However, I can guarantee you I learned that there's absolutely no substitute for hard work no matter what you do.

I know that probably sounds corny. But I don't give a fuck.

There's never been anything wrong with rolling your sleeves up and getting to work, no matter what you do for a living, no matter how much you have in life.

Better yet, I learned things I never knew about my dad during those Sunday mornings, one of them being that you can never go wrong with an incredible work ethic, that getting something done the right way was tantamount, no matter how much time or effort it took.

But it also taught me that I never wanted to clean another goddamn milk truck as long as I lived.

And I never did.

My mom took a much different approach, making sure from an early age that I would share her love of reading. She pushed harder on that than any teacher I ever had in grade school.

Probably three or four times a year she would take me to downtown Chicago on the old IC line, getting off at the Randolph St. station, a place full of sights and sounds, including the display of rotisserie chickens that always looked done to a golden turn, kind of like my old friend David Schuster.

This was supposed to be a shopping trip, but my mom just never seemed to be all that crazy about browsing the stores on Michigan Ave., or for that matter anywhere else.

I soon discovered that the only place she really seemed interested in was the old Kroch's and Brentano's, back then the biggest bookstore in the business.

She steered me to the Hardy Boys series and I would later make the Doc Savage books a huge part of my early reading matter. She didn't seem to mind that I would soon stretch out to the James Bond collection and then some other books that seemed well beyond my years. But I loved them all, including *Northwest Passage* by Kenneth Roberts, which remains one of my all-time favorites.

But that wide-eyed kid was about to disappear as I prepared to start at Bloom Township High School. In his place was someone who would become an ongoing problem. Not a serious problem, mind you, but one who certainly was going to veer into the underachieving lane and stay there.

My first nine years of school were marked by straight A's, until the new math in eighth grade tripped me up, as did a science class. Getting the picture here? As long as I was having things my own way, and school was a snap, I was good.

But when presented with a challenge, particularly in a subject I didn't care about, I turtled. I only think about that now, by the way. If had bothered me to screw something up, I would have done my best to make it right.

I didn't. So it was on to Bloom.

chapter 4

Is Anybody
Listening?

Sometimes the safest thing you can do when it comes to making a career decision is to not actually make one, putting me somewhere between being a wishy-washy bastard and having a fear of commitment.

So when Seth Mason called me back a week or so after our initial interview to ask if I wanted to be part of the new 820-AM family, I gave him the old yes…but.

Sure, I'd love to come aboard. But I still wasn't sure that leaving the *Sun-Times* was the right thing to do, even if they'd basically screwed me six ways from any given Sunday. Sometimes, humans want to hold on to the only safety net they've ever known. That was me.

At any rate, you might remember how different things were in that fall of '91. Newspapers weren't anywhere near the money-burning financial disasters they've become. If anything, it was the radio thing that seemed more fly-by-night, particularly for a start-up station that apparently was being powered by a family of hamsters.

I mean Mary Kay Kleist almighty, The Score was going to be on the air during the daylight hours only during the winter months, meaning that when the sun was gone at 4:30, we'd be off the air. There would also be signoff times of 5, 5:30 and 6 at various times of the year.

During the prime summer hours, the station would be on until 9 PM.

Wow. Start the freakin' parade.

But that was our lot in life because a Texas station had the sole rights to air 24-hour programming on the 820 frequency. But things weren't all bad. Because a station in Scranton, Pennsylvania, had recently closed its doors, Diamond was able to secure the call letters WSCR and The Score was born with a neat twist, getting the kind of branding that both Mason and Lee loved and needed.

That aside, it's easy to look back now and think how easy the decision should have been for me considering everything. Sorry, it just wasn't.

McNeil and I would be the alleged afternoon-drive show that was going to disappear before the vast majority of commuters even reached their cars. I'm no radio programmer, but that sounds like an afternoon show that's doomed to hit the shitter, which I believe is an old radio term for *boy are we fucked*.

Thankfully, to his everlasting credit Seth understood. There was no brow-beating, no "how about actually making a commitment." Put myself in his position and I probably would have said to make up your goddamn mind.

But Mason, ever the gentleman, didn't do that. I never really asked him if he loved the decision or loathed it, but I don't guess it's that important.

After a brief discussion, the decision was made that I would team with McNeil in the afternoons, something that would be exceedingly comfortable for me. On days when my newspaper schedule wouldn't allow me to be in the city, another *Sun-Times* man—and longtime friend—Brian Hanley, would work with McNeil.

I know the money wasn't great, especially back then when every cent mattered. I knew this whole science project wasn't about the cash, but I certainly would have loved more of it.

To supplement, Hanley and I would also work Saturday mornings together on what came to be called The Young Sportswriters which sounds funny now but worked at the time.

The bigger picture, as I was told countless times, is that we would be part of an historic moment in Chicago radio. We were going to be the pioneers in the effort to make an all-sports station a viable commodity in a fierce radio market that was nothing if not unforgiving.

We were going to try and establish something in a town flooded with radio stars, including the likes of Steve Dahl and Garry Meier, whose legendary afternoon show had set a standard by which all others were measured.

Did we have a chance in hell?

Sure. There's always a chance.

Our opening day lineup was longtime TV sports guy Tom Shaer in the morning and North and ex-Bear Dan Jiggetts in the middays. I would work with McNeil in the afternoon slot and Hanley would fill in on days when my schedule took me out of

For my final broadcast, I was joined by many familiar faces from The Score's early years (from left): Brian Hanley, Dan McNeil, Mike North, Tom Shaer, and Dan Jiggetts. *(Courtesy of 670 The Score)*

town. The eternally creepy and weird Mike Murphy was hired for weekends. He would also follow us at night depending on the time of the year. More about him later. I shiver just thinking about it.

Two other things I knew we had going for us: Chicago is an amazing sports city and Dan Lee.

I'm sure that name has been lost in all that's happened in the last 20 years or so, but it was Lee, the man who'd made 'XRT and Diamond Broadcasting into such a rousing success, that put up the cash to secure the 820 signal.

I don't know if Dan was the world's greatest sports fan at the time. It sure didn't seem like it. But I do know a smart guy and a brilliant businessman when I meet one and that was him.

Short and stocky, Lee's blunt sense of humor could occasionally rub some the wrong way, although that was never the case with me.

I remember feeling exhilarated the first time we met. He made you think this whole sports thing was going to be a radio revolution, that we were going to succeed and let the critics (we'd hear plenty from them) be damned.

Is it possible to believe in what someone is saying yet still feel like you needed a blindfold and a cigarette?

I promise you that's exactly the way I felt on Jan. 2, 1992, the day The Score officially came into existence.

IT'S A FUNNY thing about on-air chemistry.

Whether it be TV or radio or theater or any other form of the arts, it's something you can't buy, no matter how much money you have.

They say shit happens. Well, so does chemistry.

I mention this only because while it was true I had done some shows with McNeil, there was certainly no guarantee that we could carry it off on a continuing basis.

First of all, he was the only true radio guy amongst us. What I actually knew about the art of radio when I started at The Score wasn't much, despite having some experience.

Here's what I understood. When the light goes on, say something, fuckface.

Not much depth there.

But then I hardly consider myself a deep thinker, which I suppose drew me to sports in the first place.

So there I was trying to learn as we went along and also trying to avoid the moments when Mount McNeil showed up.

His occasional fits of pique generally included something being picked up and thrown. And Danny could wing it with the best of them.

Then there was our first executive producer Judd Sirott. While he's a sweetheart of a guy I still love to death, back then Judd was a bundle of nervous energy and intensity that would often spill out into our yet-to-be-hallowed hallways. Youthful enthusiasm can still take you a long way in most businesses and Judd had a ton of it.

So did midday producer Jesse Rogers. On more than one occasion in the early days of the station, the two of them would get into it over guests. The ours-yours tug of wars could be heard in many parts of the building, and neither was going to give an inch. Territorial? Oh, yeah. Crazy? Yes. There was some of that as well. Plenty to go around actually. The two looked like they wanted to kill each other, but to my knowledge no blows were ever struck, despite disagreements that arose quite frequently.

Is that normal? As a matter of fact, yes. They were both highly territorial and fiercely loyal to their shows, things that must be counted on the plus side for any producer. You wanted your producer to be that guy. Someone who would have your back in any situation that might come up.

Judd did. As did every producer who followed him over the years. Maybe not quite as demonstratively, mind you, but there was never doubt where the loyalties of Mike Alzamora or Matt Fishman or Dan Zampillo or Matt Abbatacola lied, although Abbatacola made it public knowledge early on that he didn't much care for Dan Bernstein.

Anyway, as things evolved over the first year or so, it became evident to just about everyone that there were enough guests to go around. Each show would eventually find a comfort zone with certain people who would fit in seamlessly with what we were doing.

But the competitive fires between Judd and Jesse never truly burned out. From first day to last, they were both motivated and involved. Again, you can't ask for more.

Fortunately, Danny and I started to find a comfort zone in a relatively short amount of time. And that was a good thing, because you couldn't have put a piece of paper between us in the studio.

We were sitting just inches apart in the tiny makeshift studio, with McNeil right next to the root of the transmitter, which was seemingly pumping out as much as 100 watts at any given time.

That first month or so was also memorable for its solitude. I can remember sitting around waiting for someone, anyone to call, even it was a wrong number or a heavy breather. Danny would give the number out over and over and over again with little or no reaction.

How many calls did we get in that first month or so?

Too few to mention, but it seemed like about six. Maybe seven.

Worse, after the first three months of ghost town radio, Robert Feder of the *Sun-Times* got himself a big headline on his radio-TV column when he gleefully announced that The Score's ratings were 0.00.

My first reaction was *oh, fuck,* sending me immediately to the offices of both Mason and Lee, where I just wanted to get some kind of positive feedback, no easy trick considering 0.00 isn't much to work with. Seth, I remember, told me to put that ratings stuff out of my mind, that everything would be okay. That would be the first of many trips to that office. Same for Lee, who didn't equivocate that day in the least. "We're not going anywhere," he said. "We've got all the time in the world. Just keep that in mind."

My second reaction was *fuck Feder* for his sense of glee (at least that's what I took it to be), especially a few days later when he wrote a tiny retraction saying his numbers were wrong, that people actually were listening. This is a guy I'd known from the *Sun-Times* and I recalled the two of us walking back to the paper after The Score had thrown a welcoming party for the media at Harry Caray's downtown restaurant just before we went on the air.

Feder couldn't have been more of a gentleman, saying he was pulling for me, adding that he expected me to succeed because I was a funny guy.

Funny how? I only ask because those were the last kind words I ever heard from him on any level, not that I was expecting any hosannas or bouquets.

For some reason, known only to himself, Feder always seemed to take exceptional pleasure in kicking The Score around back then. Now I'm not suggesting we couldn't have used a good, swift kick in the ass at times. We more than deserved it. Feel free to pick a reason, any reason.

But even at that, it also suggests those words he had for me on that long-ago night couldn't have been more disingenuous.

Look, if you want to say I'm a worthless asswipe, feel free. I've heard it more than once, but don't say one thing to my face and then take such glee at the station's troubles—and mine—just a few scant months later.

Besides, any critic should certainly understand that three months isn't exactly what you'd call a big sample size, plus we were basically fighting with one arm tied behind our backs and the other dragging in the dirt.

I also learned years later that being big buddies with a TV-radio critic isn't a bad way to go, that forming a tight, personal relationship can lead to some great things being written about you, while the other guy, aka the competition, is a douchebag. In case you haven't guessed, I was the Bag.

I've since learned to roll with the punches, letting the critics take their best shots. Hey, if you're going to dish it out as I always have, you'd better be able to take it and I think I can.

Besides, the real fun at The Score, including plenty of controversy, wasn't that far off.

chapter 5

Bob

I'm going to date myself a bit here, but years ago *Reader's Digest* ran an enormously popular series called "The Most Unforgettable Character I Have Ever Met." Some of you might remember the halcyon days of the publication when it was published in 32 editions in 13 languages and claimed to have more 100 million readers.

The vast majority of you probably don't. But if you look real hard, you'll still find the publication exists even today, although the circulation numbers aren't quite as gaudy as they were decades ago when the *RD* was king.

So who is the most unforgettable person you've ever met? Could be your mom or dad, a road many chose to take. A sibling. Maybe a friend or a teacher or someone you worked with. The possibilities were endless, and most avenues were explored more than once.

I mention this not only to give the series its props, but because I have no other way on earth to introduce you to Bob Aebi, my Bloom High School classmate, and the guy who would bring me into several adventures, opening my rather cloistered world to some of the craziest people and goofiest times I would ever have in my life.

But let's start from the beginning of what today would be referred to as a bromance.

Although we'd grown up only a few miles apart, we'd never met until gym class of our junior year after we'd shifted from the new Bloom on Sauk Trail to the old Bloom in Chicago Heights. Hard to believe I didn't remember even seeing Bob in the hallways in my first two years, but that freshman year had been one of the most unsettling, disturbing times of my life. I felt like had completely failed during that 1964-65 school year, that my test scores coming out of eighth grade were luck more than anything else. How else to explain such a terrible freshman year when I could have been declared MIA.

There was really no missing Aebi. He was 6'5", weighed a rather robust 280 pounds and that was topped off by a mop of black, curly hair that made him more more distinct, as if he needed it.

And he was country strong as I would soon observe. In short, he was the kind of guy who would have been voted most likely to have the varsity football coach chasing him down in the hallways on a daily basis.

Not that Bob would have even stopped. He wasn't really interested in football or playing much of anything else at that time. The one thing you made sure of in Bob's company is that he didn't flip that switch he had. He could go from calm, mild-mannered Bob, to Big, Bad, Angry Bob in an instant. I can still vividly recall the day he put my lifelong friend Mike Downey in a choke hold, or sleeper hold if you will. Mike must have turned five different shades of red before Bob let him go.

I remember my response was something to the tune of, "Holy shit, Bob, take it easy."

It's the best I could come up with.

Mike was okay, but not all that sure of what had just happened. I was certain from that moment on that I would never screw with Bob, but the occasion would never arise. I don't recall even so much as a cross word between the of two us. We were alike on many levels, the only difference being that he could probably kill you with his bare hands and about all I could do was bore you to death.

Not long after that, Bob and I would be spending practically every day together. He wasn't a huge sports fan, but that was fine. I had plenty of friends who were.

Like most children of the 1960s, we shared similar tastes in music. We would spend hours at his house on weekends, listening to The Beatles, The Stones, The Dave Clark Five, et al. We'd break down every song, every lyric, what we liked and what we didn't like. What we thought it meant. I recall that "Louie Louie" by The Kingsmen was a particular favorite, even though it had first come out in 1963.

According to some, the lyrics, if you listened closely, were rather filthy for that day or any other day. The argument from the other side was that while the lyrics were a bit weird and at times hard to decipher, there was nothing dirty about the song. I get it. I also chose to hear what I wanted to hear—the dirty ones. *Oh, baby, I say a way down low.*

"Louie Louie" has since been called the song with the "foulest lyrics never written."

Whatever. At least I didn't get hooked on porn. At that point, I hadn't even been hooked on a feeling.

Not long after we met, Bob told me he'd taken a job at the Trail Room restaurant in the old Marshall Fields in Park Forest. I had just turned 16 at the time, still walking everywhere and getting a few bucks a week for doing a little busywork at a gas station near Dixie Dairy in the Heights.

When Bob offered to put in a good word for me, I was all for it. How could I turn down the riches of a $1.25 per hour? That was minimum wage at the time, but if I was ever going to get a car, now was the time to start saving.

Yeah, I know, at that pay scale it would have taken approximately 3,300 hours of work to have enough money for a decent car. And that would be without me spending a cent. There was also one other problem—I didn't even have a driver's license.

That meant that Bob, who was driving a beat-up old Chevy station wagon, would have to pick me up and take me home. He didn't mind. But then he never did. We both worked the 3 to 11 shift. On any day, you could be working as a bus boy, a dishwasher or slinging hash at the Chuck Wagon.

The Chuck Wagon seemed easy enough. All you'd have to do was throw on a chef's hat and be prepared to dish up a plate of food for kids who wouldn't be eating off the regular menu. The offering was simple, too, hot dogs and beans for the precious tykes, who were nothing if not a throbbing pain in the ass.

I think I worked the Chuck Wagon twice before my boss, Barbara, told me that I would never do it again. "You're really bad at it," she said. I knew that. I also knew busing was a seniority thing, so I wouldn't be doing that, either.

Hello dishwashing, my old friend, I've come to clean with you again.

No matter. The money was just about the same. You might get an extra buck or two busing, but the waitresses weren't necessarily known for their generosity.

Bob, meanwhile, had other plans for his money, plans that I haven't shared with you as of yet. Hey, I'm getting to it—Bob wanted to be a professional wrestler.

I admit I was shocked the first time I heard it. I'm sure Bob wasn't the first kid who'd dreamed of such things, nor would he be the last.

The first time he informed me of his intentions, I thought he was screwing with me. There's no way his mother was going to endorse such an undertaking. Turns out, she did. So did Bob's sister Corinne, who'd learned long ago to never doubt him. When he wanted something, he went after it.

And I went with him. Everywhere. We went to wrestling matches at the International Amphitheater, the Hammond Civic Center, and even took a road trip to Minneapolis where the TV show with Roger Kent announcing emanated. There were five of us in the car, including Tony "the Good" Shepherd, who was bawdy as hell and didn't care who was listening.

While Bob was getting the lay of the land during that trip, Tony was getting the lay of the night about three feet from where I was sleeping.

Now that's a weekend with a squishy center.

WHEN WE WEREN'T traveling, Bob was spending most Friday and Saturday nights at Bob Sabre's Wrestling Academy in Chicago. Sabre, the Fifth Beatle, aka George Ringo, loved what he did. He taught Bob every trick, including how to fall without killing yourself, how to sell the whole act, including the posturing.

I would occasionally be needed for something, so I wasn't a complete fifth wheel. Nothing dramatic, mind you, maybe just applying a hold or sometimes bouncing off a rope or maybe even bouncing off one of the Bobs.

Was it fun? You bet. Did I ever dream of joining Bob in the business? Not a chance. First and foremost, I don't think I could have afforded the training, and second, there would have been a line at my house to see who was going to kill me. (I would have bet on my mom.)

After those sessions with Sabre, we wouldn't go home. Not with Mr. Party at the wheel. We'd hit The Kinetic Playground, which had once been called the Electric Theater on Lawrence, where we saw various bands, including a group called Sha Na Na. If we had tickets, we'd also get over to the Aragon Ballroom, once catching Gary Puckett & the Union Gap, one of my favorites.

So there were times when the path was smooth, when everything was cool. There were other times when things turned into an absolute nightmare.

This happened after both of us had graduated Bloom and Bob, sure enough, was getting his professional career started and I was at Prairie State Junior College, taking classes that would be transferred to my intended destination, Northern Illinois University.

On one particular weekend Bob had a match in Beloit, Wisconsin. I'm pretty sure Bob, or Bulldog Drummer as he came to be called, was supposed to lose this match. That was generally what happened to guys who were referred to as "heels."

I was acting as his dipshit manager that night, something I was good at. Not managing, but being a dipshit. The match hadn't been going for very long before Bulldog had so riled up the fans with his act, some of them were even approaching the ring.

I was standing roughly two feet away from him when he gave the ropes a mighty kick. He didn't hit anybody, but a pregnant woman immediately began screaming that she'd been kicked.

That was uh-oh time.

She was lying through her teeth, but it didn't matter. The die had been cast.

After Bulldog lost, we beat a hasty retreat to the locker room, doing our best to dodge a few flying objects.

But just a few seconds later, there were fans banging on the door, demanding their pound of flesh for kicking a pregnant woman.

Fucking idiots.

I was in a panic. I'd never been in this position before, so I had no frame of reference. All I remember is thinking that door was going to fly open at any second and we were going to have to face a mob of drunken yahoos who'd banded together for a common cause.

Bob, as you might expect, was ready to take them on. Me? Not so much.

Lucky for us, the Beloit police had fought their way to the door, telling the worked-up fools to go home. I don't know if anyone was arrested, but as far I was concerned you could have jailed every fucking one of them. Dumb shits.

Aebi eventually got his own nerves under control, took a shower, and was ready to go about 45 minutes after the fact on the advice of police.

There was no one around as we made our way back to his wagon. It looked as if we'd weathered what could have been an ugly, ugly mess for all involved.

At least that's what I thought for about 20 minutes or so. It was at that point on the interstate that the car suddenly died out with no warning. We could not get it started again. Only much later would we discover that someone had put sugar in the gas tank.

So then what, you ask? We got out and walked. And walked. And walked some more. Cell phones were still a thing in the future, so we headed home, the only thing that made sense.

We probably walked for three hours or so before we were picked up by an Illinois state trooper who took us back to the car, claiming we couldn't leave the car on the side of the road.

He radioed in for a tow truck and promptly took his leave.

Now ordinarily I wouldn't have cared, but I had a midterm exam on that Monday and I couldn't miss it.

By the time I finally got home after getting a series of rides, it was Monday morning and the test was coming up in three hours. I grabbed a couple hours sleep and drove back to the Heights. Despite feeling groggy, I did just fine on the test.

But that was the last road trip Bob and I would take. About a year later he drove to my parents' house in Steger behind the wheel of a beaten up old hearse, noting that he had just signed a deal to wrestle in Seattle. As I recall, he was changing his wrestling name to The Mummy and he would be wheeled into every match in casket, which was safely tucked in the rear of the hearse.

A little more than 20 years would pass before I saw Bob again, and it just happened to be at Bloom's 21st reunion for the class of 1968.

We'd both been married for a number of years, but Bob, who'd changed his last name to Alebi for wrestling purposes, wasn't doing particularly well.

He said he suffered a severe back injury when he'd fallen through the ring at the old Cobo Arena in Detroit several years earlier. Bob, who had his wife with him, said he'd been married a while (me, too), but times were tough.

He said he and his wife supplemented their income by rolling drunks in Toledo. I couldn't tell if he was serious or kidding. And I didn't ask.

Moments later he excused himself, returning with a giant (and I do mean giant) bowl of weed, strictly for medical purposes, of course.

I remember we all had fun that night, although the number of attendees had dwindled down to fewer than 150 Bloom grads. I couldn't shake the feeling that this didn't feel quite like it should have, that the pure joy we used to share had somehow faded over the years, due in no small part to the realities of life.

It wasn't either of our faults, really. If you don't feel the same, you don't feel the same. I had four kids and was into my second year as a *Sun-Times* columnist, a fact that didn't seem to interest Bob in the least.

I haven't seen Bob since, nor have I been able to get any additional information about what's happened to him.

But you'll never kill the memories and time hasn't diminished them in the least.

Unforgettable, indeed.

chapter 6

Ditka

Even though The Score was far from a rousing ratings success for the first six or so months, by August of '92 there were plenty of signs that the station wasn't going away anytime soon, despite those discouraging early returns.

Would it ever be a Chicago powerhouse like a WGN or WLS?

I didn't think so, but it had clearly started to find its niche with the highly desirable male 25- to 54-year-old demographic, which brings in plenty of advertising dollars.

God, I love it when I talk radio lingo.

Anyway, at least that's what I was told.

Given those assurances and the relentless prodding of McNeil and the sound advice of my lifelong friend Mike Downey, I finally made the commitment to go full time eight months into the station's existence, taking the ultimate plunge in August of '92.

I don't recall if I was happier to get a $15,000 a year bump in pay from The Score, or to put the *Sun-Times* behind me. I suppose it doesn't much matter all these years later, and I certainly don't mean to sound bitter towards the *Sun-Times*, which had been my employer since 1980.

It's just that there were no challenges left in the newspaper business. I'd gone from a lowly desk guy to covering the Bulls beat to doing features to writing a column in 12 years. Truth is, even though I'm often labeled a failed columnist and someone who was fired by the *Sun-Times* by those who don't know shit, my accomplishments in newspapers remain my proudest professional achievement.

Besides, I wasn't exactly sure that I was all that good at the whole radio thing anyway.

It would be nice to say that I was natural, that it all came easy.

I knew better. I had received enough negative feedback to understand that I was a work in progress at best, that learning the business was going to be a necessity. I could still be myself, but plenty of fine-tuning was necessary.

Perhaps luckily, the afternoon show wasn't getting much attention, which bothered Danny more than it did me, especially in the early days.

As correctly predicted by Mason, North jumped from his hot dog stand to stardom in a matter of weeks along with Jiggetts, who was also known to take his stances, just not at the same volume.

From Day One, North spoke at his own special decibel level, which immediately made people take notice. It also propelled the "Monsters of the Midday," as they would come to be called, to a notoriety that none of the other shows could approach.

"It was us against the world," Danny would often say, meaning that the reaction to our presence from the other forms of media was often negative. "Try to get ratings when you're saying good-night at 4:45."

I loved his combative spirit and sometimes even his temper tantrums, where things would often be flying through the air.

And I don't want to leave out his battles with Seth. Danny didn't think their clashes were that bad. They were to the rest of us, although whatever Danny did, he did with our best interests at heart.

WHILE THERE'S NO denying that North had a huge hand in putting the station on the map in those early years, I'm not sure that would have been enough were it not for the smartest hire the station ever made—Bears coach Mike Ditka.

Bringing his show aboard solidified that The Score was for real. And it didn't hurt that Ditka, who was fired by the Bears on Jan. 5, 1993 following a 5-11 season, had stopped talking to all other forms of media.

Quite a tumble for a guy who had ridden roughshod in the '80s, capturing the Bears' only Super Bowl victory and becoming a legend in the process, making his fall from grace an even steeper one.

But it also made tapes of the Ditka show a hot commodity around the country. They all waited for sound bites of the show to be sent their way and Ditka rarely disappointed, digging in his heels despite the team's moribund state.

Talk about fireworks.

And it would also turn out to be the place where Ditka chose to settle some personal grudges with me. I never asked to host his show and I never really had the desire to do so. But Ron Gleason, The Score's first program director, wanted me to do it. So, reluctantly, I did in the interest of being a good soldier.

And it was something. Kind of like a suicide mission, only less fun.

It had been just a few years earlier that Ditka's wife, Diana, had walked up to me in the hallway outside the Bears' locker room after a loss to the Redskins in Washington D.C. and informed me I was real "cocksucker."

Alrighty, then. At least I knew where I stood in the Ditka family. But that was just the prelude.

I'll get back to Ditka, but here's what was nice. All the media people who hated us, and the line continued to grow, had to at the very least acknowledge our existence, albeit through clenched teeth.

Longtime newspaper columnist Mike Downey has been a friend for more than 60 years.

We'd somehow become the loud-mouthed renegades of sports talk, antagonizing many just for the sake of antagonizing, according to our critics. In the current climate, if you want to be a contrarian and a complete fool, you might be worth $5 million a year from Fox. Just remember to say it like you believe it…and please scream it. That wasn't true, but that's what the perception was by many.

Here's what was true in the case of Ditka. Despite all the accolades, the Super Bowl win, and the personal fortune he was raking in with both hands, the guy remembered everything I'd ever written about him. And he didn't like any of it. He wasn't my only critic, but he was certainly the most enthusiastic and his wife was riding shotgun.

So I knew the on-air clash was about to come before too long. I can't remember if we even said hello to one another before the first show we did together. But I'm guessing not. We rarely spoke before airtime and never afterwards.

Then the magic moment finally came when I pointed out to Ditka that he seemed "resigned to his fate," answering media questions with a seeming passiveness that was uncharacteristic for a guy who was about as combative as it gets.

That did it. I'm sure the toxic combination of me, the rotten season, and his generally gruff demeanor led to "Well, you're the same guy who wrote about me when I did have the fire, that it was the wrong thing to do, so who ya crappin?" I tried to interject a thought at the point, but it was no use. But if you ever heard Who Ya Crappin' on The Score, you know that.

As Harvey Wells, a longtime Diamond exec put it on my final show, "You rode that thing for 25 years." Yes, I did. Guilty as hell. And while there were times when the bit morphed into something both hideous and bizarre, it was really, really great at times, such as when Dan Bernstein and I did it for the last time in December of 2016.

Here's the other thing. I don't recall writing any such column about Ditka, unless you put a bunch of them together and that's fine. I thought of him as a big blowhole in general and I haven't changed my mind, so the specifics don't matter.

I'll say this for Ditka, that '85 championship continues to be part of the discussion, mainly because the Bears seemingly have gotten worse and worse since their only other Super Bowl appearance in February 2006, but that's what happens when you've been a participant just twice in the 51 Super Bowls played to date. I'm pretty sure that 1-for-51 thing should be embarrassing, unless you're Tim Tebow.

And whether Ditka loved The Score, hated The Score or really didn't give a damn one way or another, in my mind his contributions to the station can't be overlooked or underestimated.

I've been asked many times why The Score ultimately succeeded, and I've gone back to Ditka whenever asked for this simple fact—I cannot be sure the station would have succeeded without him. Sure, I think it probably would have made it, but Ditka was the big name then. Plenty of people still hung on his every word, even if some of them made absolutely no sense. Fans couldn't get enough of his stories, of his tough-guy image and his permanent blue collar.

Ditka perpetuated his tough-guy legend with each Score appearance, including the call from the infamous Neal from Northlake, whose willingness to challenge Ditka as a coach led to Ditka giving him the address at Halas Hall and telling Neal to drop by, adding, "I'll whip your ass." We replayed that roughly a billion times, as did every other show on the station.

I want to say it was a number of years later when we finally met Neal in person, recognizing his voice immediately. I don't know if we'd ever see him a second time, but I can assure you that Ditka would have whipped his ass. Soaking wet, Neal probably didn't weigh 150 pounds.

As for Ditka, I used to get asked all the time if we ever managed to get past our longtime feud and become at least cordial.

Not really. I cannot envision the day when we will we ever be friends. But I have always been more than willing to give him his props about his place in the station's history and that will never change.

On that, I won't crap you.

Nor will I step back from the pure enjoyment I got from Ditka's years as coach of the New Orleans Saints, where he would trade all of his picks for Texas running back Ricky Williams in 1999.

Was Ditka high? No. But wait, Williams was. But Ditka was in desperation mode after going 6–10 in each of his first two years in New Orleans, hardly inspiring numbers for the human hot-air balloon.

And all of it was predictable, at least for me.

I don't know how many believed that Ditka would turn the Saints into winners based purely on his penchant for tough talk and no-nonsense style. But Bill Parcells he wasn't. His magic, such as it was, couldn't transform bad into good, unless all circumstances were at the optimum as they were when he took over the Bears with an enormously strong core of terrific players.

That's no different than most coaches. But I don't believe Ditka thought of himself as most coaches. Being particularly humble was not a strength. Kind of like football's version of Phil Jackson.

Jackson took over the Bulls' job at exactly the right time, riding the coattails of GOAT Michael Jordan to six NBA titles with Bulls. He would later cash in five more championships with Los Angeles Lakers teams dripping with talent, including Shaq and Kobe Bryant. And he has the hat and rings to prove it.

If Dennis Martinez was El Presidente, Jackson was Hell Presidente when he took over as the New York Knicks boss in 2014, getting a five-year $60 million gift from fuck stick owner James Dolan, who gives stupid a bad name.

When Jackson was finally—and mercifully—launched on June 29, 2017, the Knicks had gone 80-166, meaning that each New York victory during his tenure was worth about $750,000. Even Dolan isn't that dumb not to see the truth, although he is paying off the remainder of Jackson's deal.

As if the first two years of his tenure weren't bad enough, Jackson brought in Derrick Rose and signed the battered Joakim Noah to a $72 million deal before the 2016-17 season, moves that cannot be accounted for by anyone with a functioning brain.

At least the Zen Master can stop being called the When Master. It's never going to happen. How much this tarnishes Jackson's record is more than likely minimal. His defenders (there are some, right?) can certainly say that nobody can do any better given the circumstances, that Dolan is a handicap no one can bear.

If that's your side of the argument, stick with it.

At least Ditka, who didn't survive his 3-13 season in 1999, admitted at one point that he didn't "have it anymore" just about three weeks after yelling at reporters for asking him why he was in such a bad mood all the time when the team was in the 2–7 dumpster.

The Saints had lost 10 of 11 when Ditka let it be known that the team would be better off with someone else coaching the next season, carefully noting that God had probably put him in this situation to be humbled.

That humbling part didn't last long, nor do most Chicagoans seem to even care about his Bayou pratfall, just as I don't care about Jackson's face plant.

But I loved Ditka's downfall then and I love it to this very day.

And none of it changes what he did for The Score.

chapter 7

Life in the Fast Lane

It was a gorgeous summer morning in July of 2009 when I made a right turn off U.S. 30 onto Western Ave. and headed south to 26th Street.

I make that exact trip maybe three times a year or so, heading to my dentist's office in Steger.

But somehow that morning, for whatever reason, was different. Maybe it was because I would be turning 60 in a year or so, maybe it was something I ate. Don't know. But I suddenly found myself in the grip of this odd nostalgia thing, noting that this particular stretch of road, which was once so much a part of my hallowed youth, looked like shit.

Never mind that I'd known this for several years.

It was hardly a newsflash that the economy had exacted a huge toll on parts of Chicago Heights and Park Forest, just as it did on countless cities and towns across the country.

Thing is, I don't really know how much the pinch of the recession had to do with it. That's a kind way of saying I'm not sure that the Heights or Park Forest had been going in the right direction long before 2008 arrived.

There I was passing the spot where the first McDonald's in the South Suburbs once stood. Behind that Mickey D's, which remains to this day the only McDonald's I ever saw close, there used to be a miniature golf course called Pat's Wee Putt, which was a name not a condition.

Anyway, I hadn't thought of that place in years. But the tour inside my head was just beginning.

Not even a mile farther down on the left-hand side of the road was the spot where Dandy's Drive-In once stood, our '60s mecca for fast cars, dopey teenagers and, upon rare occasion, someone who actually went in just for the food.

If you've ever seen *American Graffiti* you know what I'm talking about here.

I'd spent countless hours at the place in the summer of '69, nursing a small Coke and deciding if I had enough money to take somebody up on an offer for a drag race.

The part I'm leaving out here is that my first car was a bright red '69 Dodge Charger R/T with a 440 engine. And it would fly. I mean F-L-Y. So much so it would frighten just about everyone who rode with me.

Oh, wait a minute, it was actually my driving that scared them, but I kind of enjoyed it.

Anyway, Dandy's was the place to go if you wanted a little action. There was never a shortage of muscle cars on any night of the week, including Corvettes, Mustangs, GTOs, Road Runners, you name it.

Did they all want to play? Probably. I do know I got hustled out of $50 one night by an older guy who seemed to indicate that he was going to race me in this sorry-ass looking Plymouth, only to show up out on the expressway with a fire-breathing monster of a Barracuda that ate me up.

Only later would someone tell me about the con, adding that 'Cuda was turning in the low 10s at the drag strip and was never taken out of the garage except when there was money to be made.

Lesson learned.

Anyway, just a bit farther down Western is the place where the late Wes Mason's bar once stood.

The longtime basketball coach at Bloom High School is one of my 10 favorite guys of all-time. Wes introduced me to the wonderful world of not only drinking all night, but actually being able to stay and sleep it off. This came after I had turned 21. After all, friends don't let friends drive when the situation warrants. Believe me, it warranted.

Just before I reached 26th Street there were more boarded-up buildings that took up an entire corner and even a couple of fast-food restaurants closer to the road were closed and quickly falling into a state of disrepair.

Funny thing is I didn't think about any of it on the way home, even though I took the exact same route.

I do know my appointment at the dentist had gone just fine and I still love thinking about that old Charger.

I'm not sure that a first car is that big of a deal to kids today. Maybe it still is to some. But there's no denying that millions of Baby Boomers still love those old cars just as much as I do.

Especially the first one. And especially that if only by the grace of God do you comprehend how lucky you are to still be here. But it's better here to start from the beginning.

I'D BEEN WAITING for this day in 1969 forever. By that time I had gone more than seven years without transportation of any kind after my bike had been stolen, and my dad would never in a million years have allowed me to take his car anywhere. In fact, I didn't even ask. He'd told me that a lot of things were going to happen in the next couple of years, but using his car, a gold Dodge Polara, wasn't going to be one of them.

And that was well before I even proved I was a lousy driver.

I should have had a hint of how it was going to go when I took driver's education at Bloom during my junior year. For people of a certain age, you might remember that part of the classroom preparation was to watch a movie called *Signal 30*. It was bloody and graphic, showing the twisted remains of cars that had been in some horrific accidents. It even had a picture of a steel girder that had gone through the chest of a truck driver, who had allegedly been driving too fast for conditions on a mountainy road.

Pardon me here, but that image has stuck in my memory for all these years, even though I never thought about it when I was behind the wheel.

My driving instructor was Verl Sell, who would go on to become Bloom's varsity football coach and later served as a Big Ten basketball referee for several seasons.

To say Sell wasn't sold on my driving would be an understatement, probably having something to do with the day I turned a corner way too early and hit a mailbox.

I attributed that to a lack of experience. Remember, back then, at least in my house, your parents didn't have a damn thing to do with your driving. It was your problem. What little experience I had was at the wheel of Walter Ladowski's old car. Everybody called him Haywoman, although I can't remember why. To say it wasn't extensive training would be fair. I drove a couple of blocks here and there, but Walter was no idiot. He knew when to say when.

I was perfect on the written test, but when the big day came for the road test I failed. Why? Because I hit a few cones while attempting to parallel park. That's all it took. I was done, at least for that day.

Not the end of the world, right? Depends on who you ask. I knew I would get my license sooner or later, but it would have to be at the Illinois driver's license facility in Kankakee, which, at the time, was the closest one to Steger.

To say my dad was unhappy would be an understatement. In those pre I-57 days, Kankakee was somewhat of a slog, but my dad acted as if he was being asked to drive to California.

It is against that backdrop that I failed the driver's test for a second time. This time I'd only hit one cone, but the end result was the same—no license.

I don't think my dad said three words all the way home. I know this because I didn't say anything. For one of the few times in my life I was out of things to say. I wasn't quite ready financially for the car yet, but I had saved up a fair amount.

And the thing was, the next time I took the driver's test I would have to do it without practicing parallel parking even once. To be safe, I waited a month before I broached the topic with my dad, who was still acting as if he were still in the recovery stage from the last trip.

By the time we made it back to Kankakee for the third try, it was exactly 35 days from the second attempt.

Despite feeling the pressure all the way down in the pit of my stomach, I finally made it through the parallel parking stage with the exact same guy who'd tested me on the previous trip. "Better," he said. "But if I were you, I'd avoid the parallel parking thing if possible."

I can honestly say that years went by before I ever had to try parallel parking again, and I made it without so much as a scratch on the car, which by that time had turned into a 1962 Dodge Dart with a push-button transmission.

So what happened to the Charger? More like what didn't happen to the Charger.

BACK IN THE late '60s, just about everyone who cared about cars knew about Mr. Norm's Grand Spaulding Dodge on 3300 W. Grand Ave. in Chicago. It was the mecca for those who couldn't get enough speed, who wanted to make their cars faster and faster. And Mr. Norm spent plenty of advertising dollars letting you know about the very special things he was offering to a burgeoning market.

My dad, being my dad, wanted me first to look at the Chargers at the Dodge dealership in Chicago Heights. It was a no go. About the only Charger that interested me had the storied Hemi engine, but that ran the cost to about $600 more than I'd saved.

It was on to Mr. Norm's the next weekend—and it was everything an obviously goofy kid could have wanted. I recall the showroom being enormous, jam-packed with all kinds of goodies, one faster than the other.

From this seemingly endless sea of steel and muscle, I finally found the red R/T with the 440 engine for right around what I'd saved—$3,300.

In an apparent generous mood, my dad agreed to pay the taxes on the car and he would pick up the cost of insurance until I could pay him back.

And so began the most idiotic stretch of my life, a period when all common sense would abandon me, when the lack of maturity and judgment could have easily cost me my life or someone else's.

I've spent a good amount of my adult life beating myself up over those days, even in full understanding that a teenager's brain isn't fully formed, that bouts of such madness are more the rule than the exception, also understanding that I wasn't the first (and won't be the last) kid to do stupid things behind the wheel.

With my beloved Dodge Charger at Carolyn's house in 1969.

Here's a list of the lowlights.

- I spent about $1,500 more on the car to add various performance parts, including what amounted to racing slicks put on the back. I am also convinced those parts were probably stolen, unless you think that a garage in the middle of an Indiana cornfield was legit. My first hint was that the price was more than reasonable, the second was that the place didn't have what you'd call office hours. You needed a recommendation from a friend to get in the garage door. As it happened, I knew a guy who knew a guy. My appointment was for 10 PM.

    I had barely gotten used to the newfound muscle when I took the car and parked it at the old Washington Park in Homewood, right under just about the brightest streetlight you could find in the lot. Betting only small amounts at the time, I was around $40 ahead when Carolyn and I returned to the car—or not.

    My baby was gone. I knew I was in the right spot by the right light. I also knew I was fucked, I just didn't know how badly. Anyway, the car was finally found about five days later. It was up on blocks on the South Side of Chicago. Tires gone, the new gear gone, basically stripped of everything that mattered, including my dignity.

    That's why you have insurance, right? Well, sorta. My insurance company at the time said they would not replace the extras that had been added to car, that I would get the stock tires, transmission, etc. that came off the showroom floor, nothing more. That they would eventually cancel me didn't bother me. That another of the major insurers would also cancel me a few years later didn't faze me either, but that was yet to come. Not that I hold a grudge or anything, but I've had absolutely no dealings with one of the insurers since then.

- Every so often, particularly early on, I would take the car out to Route 30 Dragstrip, where you could go as fast as you wanted. I never turned in any quarter time that was mind-numbing, generally getting home in somewhere in the low 14s. With the parts I once had, it probably would have turned somewhere in the mid 13s. But that's just a guess based on talking to other drivers. But I didn't care. During one of my infrequent trips, I had the opportunity to meet Big Daddy Don Garlits, aka The Godfather of drag racing. He was driving the Swamp Rat XIII, a slingshot rail. He would later suffer what was termed a catastrophic failure in 1970 when the transmission Garlits was developing blew during a race. The injuries he suffered put him out for the rest of the season. I was luckier, if that's what you want to call it. During the last race I ever had at 30, I blew a piston (not a Piston) and needed to have the car towed back home. My dad, despite bitching just about every step of the way, bought the necessary parts and fixed it. And I paid for it in just about every sense of the word. Did I learn a lesson? Not really.

- Aside from the almost daily troubles with the Steger police, my next incident scares me to this day. I was driving south on Chicago Rd., heading home after spending time at Carolyn's. We were about a half a block from Dixie Dairy when the guy in front of me stopped his car right in the middle of the street. I didn't see anything wrong, so I swung around him to the left lane to pass. Thank my lucky stars I didn't step on it. I hadn't gone much more than 15 feet when I saw a kid crossing the street on my right-hand side. I smashed the brakes, but it was too late. I caught him with the right side of my bumper. When I got to him he was clearly in pain, moaning that I'd hit his left leg. The rest is a blur. I could barely think straight. The Chicago Heights cops showed up and then came the ambulance. We were only a mile or so from St. James Hospital, and the kid's injuries weren't life-threatening. But there I was, in the midst of a bunch of people who were giving me the skunk eye, probably because the Charger was still running and rumbling in the street. When I learned the next day that the 11 year old had suffered a broken leg, I went to the hospital for a visit, just to make sure he was okay. He looked even smaller in the bed, but when I asked if he knew who I was, he said, "You hit me with a Super Bee." No, I told him I hit you with a Charger. The ticket I got that night for failing to yield the right of way to a pedestrian was later dismissed in court when it was established the guy driving the car in front of me that night had stopped to signal the kid to cross the street. I hadn't seen that. I had dodged what could have been a life-altering circumstance. But that Dodge couldn't dodge what came next.

- When you enjoyed street racing, the most important thing to do was find an appropriate spot, one that wasn't well-traveled after about 9 PM. The spot of choice for the Dandy's crowd was roughly seven to ten miles away, almost to Indiana. Not only was the isolation good, but there was even a pull-off spot on the road that probably held about 20 cars when full. But on this night, this race was set up with one of my best friends at the time, who had a Plymouth Road Runner. We wound up going a little over 140 mph, side by side. Although there was absolutely nothing at stake, I wasn't letting off. Neither was he. But I took it too far. Finally remembering that a major intersection was coming up in just a moment or two, I hit the brakes, hoping I wasn't too late. My bad. There was a distinct smell of something burning, but I didn't think about that, I just wanted to stop before the light, which was red. I did manage to finally stop, but I knew I'd done something with the panic move. I mentioned to my dad the next day that the brakes just didn't feel right. He gave me that look, but took the car to the Dixie Dairy garage a day later. He wound up replacing the brake drums with power brake drums. I had no idea what that meant. But the car was okay now. The explosion I expected from him never came, unless you consider him repeating that he wasn't my goddamn pit crew. One other thing you should know about all of this: I never wore a seatbelt. Neither did any of my friends. I don't even remember if the car had seatbelts of any kind.

- When I worked the night shift at the Jack-in-the-Box in Chicago Heights, I kept the Charger parked right behind the back door of the place, making sure that if anyone was in a mind to race, I'd be happy to oblige. Wait, I was working, right? Technically, yes. But I could get away for a few minutes if need be. Besides, when we'd get a line of cars wanting food approaching closing time of midnight, I'd simply turn off the outside lights and say we were in the process of locking it down. So, no, I wouldn't have been missed for a half hour or so. You probably had a better chance of getting food if I wasn't there. I want to say I was challenged about five times during my Jack years, including one snowy night when I took three 50-pound bags of salt and threw them in the trunk for added traction. It didn't work. I couldn't get any traction that night and got wiped out by a car I would have easily beaten in optimum conditions. All told, I was 3–2 in those runs, clearing a whole $20. Was it worth it? Oh, yeah.

• It was early in the start of the 1970-71 school year. I had gotten my two years in at Prairie State and was now at Northern Illinois University. And so was the Charger. I'd found a downstairs room in a DeKalb house along with two other guys. We'd gotten along well enough to sit around a cartoonishly small TV to watch the first Monday Night Football game ever played on Sept. 20, 1970. It was the New York Jets vs. the Cleveland Browns. So far so good. I actually liked the first roomies of my life. But for me, trouble was never too far away. I'd been told that the DeKalb police were not fond of fast cars, that they took no shit when it came to driving. So I slowed down. At least I thought I did. I was giving a friend of a friend a ride back to his place because he'd been a tad overserved. I was sober. Good thing. I had dropped him off at his apartment and was trying to figure out a way back to our place. About three blocks later—they all look the same when you're lost—I suddenly saw a little white car to my left pulling out of a driveway. Apparently he never saw me. I swerved right, and I swear for God that I wasn't going that fast by my standards. That's an argument that I would have never been able to prove. As I veered right, I had all of about 10 feet before I hit the first parked car. That was quickly followed by a second, a third, a fourth, a fifth, a sixth, a seventh, and an eighth. I just couldn't get control, basically because at first impact the right side fender had been driven into my right front tire. That will keep you bouncing. By the time I came to a stop, the car had filled with smoke and I wasn't feeling well at all. In a matter of moments, my car was surrounded by a swarm of little old ladies. I thought I was hallucinating, but I was not. What I had so rudely done was sideswipe almost all of their cars parked for their weekly bingo party. And I was actually more embarrassed than hurt, especially because they seemed to care more about how I was doing than the damage I had wrought. The bottom line is that the insurance bill to fix all the damage came to more than $4,000 (cheap by today's standards) and, once again, the second of the two giant insurance companies canceled me. That one I got.

IT WOULD BE decades before I drove a high-performance car again and my driving record is damn near spotless. And, yes, I feel a helluva lot luckier than that punk who was staring down the barrel of Dirty Harry's giant pistol on the streets of San Francisco way back in the '70s.

Here's the truth. That Charger was more than likely unsafe at any speed. So was just about every other car on the road, except for the few I'll give the putt-putt exception. That's not a golfing term. Where cars have come in the last 50 years or so is incredible, both in safety and performance, although I must say the thought of those faulty driver's side air bags exploding in your face gives me pause. So do the so-called distracted drivers, who literally wouldn't put their own phone down to save their lives. And, yes, this is coming from me.

But don't even try to say you haven't seen one of those shit-for-brains fucks out there driving with only one eye on the road and sometimes maybe only half of that. And you have to keep in mind how many more vehicles are out there now than there ever have been. To put in one word: terrifying.

chapter 8

The Trial of the Century

As we began year four at The Score in 1995, I was finally beginning to feel a bit more at ease. I know that the ratings weren't what anyone would call shiny and sparkling, but the partnership with Danny was working out great and I was finally beginning the process of making sure that every day was going to be fun. I felt as if I was getting better at the craft and our transitions with North and Jiggetts had become must-listen-to radio, or at least so I was told.

Made sense really. North always seemed to have plenty to say when 2 PM rolled around, and he generally said it in a loud and self-assured tone. Did it always make sense? Not that I recall, but it never seemed to matter. He'd told me once that I didn't know more about Illinois basketball than he did just because I'd seen Deon Thomas naked. That's a good line, but the problem was I'd never even been in the Illini locker room because it was off-limits to the media and I hadn't seen Deon showering in the hallway. Still, a funny line is a funny line. As for Jiggs, he was every bit as ready as North for the daily transition, just at a more reasonable decibel level.

I'll admit I wasn't sure about any of it some days, simply because at times it was just screaming for the sake of screaming, although that has become a very valuable commodity in just about any form of modern communication. For many, screaming is far more important than logic.

My reason for optimism, however, didn't have a thing to do with any of that. Nor did have anything to do with the Bears, who were sitting in a pile of awful muck. So were the Hawks and the Bulls, whose string of three straight championships would end when Michael Jordan, cloaked in a veil of rumors and innuendo regarding gambling and other matters, had left basketball.

Bulls and White Sox owner Jerry Reinsdorf, the man I had warred with on more than one occasion as a columnist, cast Jordan a lifeline when the announcement was made Jordan would play baseball with the Class AA Birmingham Barons.

That move, of course, was unprecedented at the time and I have a feeling that nothing like it will ever happen again, especially when you consider that Jordan had been busy making a compelling case to be called the greatest basketball player of all-time, a title he would later cement.

While Jordan took his share of criticism for his baseball skills, it must be noted that he was actually better than most thought he'd be. I was one of the doubters. But how could you not be? He was 31 years old, he hadn't played in more than 20 years, and being a great athlete doesn't necessarily translate into being a great baseball player. I remember that infamous *Sports Illustrated* cover picture of Jordan batting in his black Birmingham Barons jersey.

The accompanying headline was "Bag it, Michael!" Right under that: "Jordan and the White Sox are embarrassing baseball."

That created a shit storm on many levels. You see, I long ago learned that to cross Michael means you're likely to lose him forever. And as I write this, *SI* still means pure hatred to Jordan and has for more than 20 years. Now that's a grudge. It even includes a special commemorative *SI* addition in 2013 that marked Jordan's 50th birthday in spectacular fashion. Not enough to get a quote from Jordan, but spectacular nonetheless.

As for Steve Wulf, who wrote the "Bag It" story, he long ago admitted that his piece was far too critical of Jordan. You might remember that.

What you might not know is that Wulf actually visited with Jordan a second time—that's amazing in and of itself—and wound up writing a second story, carefully noting that Jordan was "showing signs" of major-league potential.

And take one guess what *SI* did? If you said they didn't run the story, you'd be correct.

You can also say this for Jordan, who professed over and over a longtime love for baseball, he was certainly setting himself up for the kind of sports failure he hadn't endured since the late '80s into 1990 when he and the Bulls couldn't find a way to beat the ass-wipe Detroit Pistons, losing three straight playoff series.

The most vivid of that three-pack of suck came in 1990 in Game 7 of the Eastern Conference Finals, a particularly galling loss at the Palace of Auburn Hills.

The big problem was that Scottie Pippen, who'd become Jordan's badly needed wing man, was suffering from a migraine headache that wouldn't allow him to play his usual big minutes, even as coach Phil Jackson exhorted him.

I was sitting right behind the Bulls bench, listening to Jackson, at least in my interpretation, trying to shame Pippen into playing more. "You ready yet Scottie?" Jackson bellowed more than once, using what certainly sounded like a sarcastic, if not downright demeaning tone.

Jackson would later deny that was his intent.

We will forever disagree on that.

When I got to Jordan in the locker room later, he wasn't worried about Pippen. His target, as usual, was general manager Jerry Krause. I asked what it would take for the Bulls to finally beat Detroit. "Go ask the fat guy in the blue shirt," Jordan huffed.

But I digress. The reason I was looking so forward to the new year was the upcoming murder trial of Orenthal James Simpson, which was set to begin on Jan. 24 in Los Angeles.

Simpson, the Hall of Fame football icon, broadcaster, pitch man, and movie star, stood accused of killing his ex-wife Nicole Brown Simpson and restaurant waiter Ron Goldman, on June 12, 1994, in a most savage fashion, leaving a trail of DNA that should have made this entire thing a slam dunk, but, of course, that's not what happened.

Here's what also didn't happen. During the entire process, both before and after the trial, none of this in any way turned out to be pleasurable for me, particularly in the tenor of calls we took.

In point of fact, it was awful, often bordering on vomit-in-ducing, as the lines were clogged throughout the course of the 11-month trail. Then came Oct. 9, 1994, when Simpson was found not guilty. The aftermath, at least to me, was hideous. Trying to argue that this trial shouldn't have had anything to do with skin color, no matter how many people only saw it that way, was a fruitless argument. The image of cheering African-Americans celebrating the verdict around the country was one that has seared itself into my memory. Let the facts of the case be damned, sort of like the Trump presidency.

My reaction was outrage, sometimes bordering on pure fury. You see, I didn't look at this entire carnival as any kind of statement about race in America as so many did. I looked at it through only one prism, as the freeing of a remorseless butcher who had literally gotten away with a senseless double murder that showed the world his true soul.

But then, I was one of those who mistakenly thought that race relations in this country had improved by the time 1995 rolled around. Could I have been any more incorrect? Uh, no.

So am I correct now, more than two decades since the Simpson verdict? It's clear that not much has changed in the ensuing 23 years. And that's just downright sad.

Oh, efforts have been made on both sides by people way smarter than I am, but I have no doubt that the feelings that continue to fester aren't going away any time soon, if ever. And even if someone told me we had at last hit a happy point, I absolutely, positively would not believe them.

Given the current climate, where the distrust of the police has perhaps hit an all-time high, I know I'm right.

Of course, I usually think I'm right. Call it a professional hazard.

As for Simpson, the fact that he's spent almost the last 10 years in prison after being found guilty of robbery and kidnapping in that bizarre Las Vegas incident does my heart good.

I know it won't bring anyone back from the dead, but it was great to see Fred Goldman, father of murder victim Ron, smile again, even admitting that his $34 million victory in the civil suit vs. Simpson was empty. More importantly, we saw during the tapes of the deposition in the civil case that Simpson was an arrogant, lying sack of shit bastard who wouldn't know the truth if it met him on the 50-yard line.

His denial of wearing the infamous Bruno Magli shoes on the night of the murder was pure folly. Simpson said he didn't own and wouldn't wear such an ugly-ass pair of shoes, even though there were all kinds of pictures of him in those U-A shoes on many occasions, including at football games when he worked for NBC covering the NFL.

I'm not going to argue that our justice system isn't highly flawed. It is. Nor am I going to say it's fair to all segments of our society. We've seen way too much to believe that.

But how can the so-called Trial of the Century end in such a manner? How do we justify such a blatant miscarriage of justice? There have always been plenty of theories, including that the jury just didn't understand the complicated case presented by Marcia Clark and Christopher Darden.

I call bullshit on that. There's a big difference between not understanding and not wanting to. The DNA evidence seemed clear enough to everyone I knew, and I don't have any forensic scientists listed in my inner circle.

That's not to say there weren't some missteps by the prosecution. There were. But were any egregious enough, including the glove, to come up with the not guilty verdict? Not in my world. Common sense, if you cared to partake, painted a much more accurate picture of what happened.

I tried to make those points during the trial. I guess I wasn't very successful. Passionate enough, but just not good enough. I learned how Clark and Darden must have felt.

There was no justice in this case, just as there were never enough good, thoughtful calls as we worked our way through that torturous year.

Amid all the O.J. tumult, there was yet another piece of news that hit The Score hallways—word had it that Lee was about to sell XRT, The Score, and a third station in Oklahoma City. The buyer: Westinghouse Broadcasting.

It seems that Lee, who'd never stopped trying to get a signal that would make The Score a 24-hour station, had heard in the latter stages of 1994 that they had finally gotten governmental permission to go 24 hours. All they needed at that point was to construct a tower that would better aim the signal.

That's when Lee had reached out to Westinghouse, asking if he could buy the 670 signal. Rather than accept the offer, Westinghouse countered by offering to buy the Diamond properties. After some rather interesting negotiations, Lee accepted the tidy sum of $77 million as a lovely parting gift.

I remember sitting in Lee's office shortly afterward, not to register a bitch as apparently some of the employees had done, but rather to offer him a heartfelt congratulations and a hug.

Unless you're presented with such a situation, it's easy to say you'd never sell your precious babies, in this case his stations.

It's also short-sighted if not downright ignorant.

You started the entire process to make money, to provide for your family. Just how in hell do you turn down the chance for generational wealth?

Lee was beaming that day. So was Mason, who was also up for a little chunk of the pie. "It's more money than I needed," Lee told me that day wearing a smile suitable for the occasion. "But I'm not complaining."

It's nice to see someone you know, love, and respect hit the jackpot, and I never, ever felt like this was some kind of betrayal on his part. The Score had established itself as a product on the rise, one to watch in the years to come.

Sure, you can sweat the idea of what happens next if you choose, but it wouldn't have been worthwhile in this case. It's a personality-driven business and many at the station had established themselves long ago.

I might be a born worrier, but I didn't waste any on this. I tipped my cap to Dan and Seth that day and I still do for a job well done.

If only the whole O.J. thing had been as easy to digest.

chapter 9

The Love of My Life

It's been said of today's millennials that many of them don't seem all that concerned about true romance. I'm aware that millions of kids today apparently are quite content to go out in groups of three or four guys and three or four girls, that one-on-one dates aren't that high on the priority list.

I can relate to that too if you take away the roving pack of friends and the dating part.

I'm not saying that I wasn't as acutely horny as every teenage boy seems to be in any generation, I just don't recall it. I'm aware that it all becomes a better story if I'm out traveling the jism trail as a kid, but I'd be lying.

The point here is how in the hell was I supposed to know the love of my life had walked into my life if I'd never been on that many dates?

With that in mind, here's the story of how I met the love of my life, not to mention my best friend, Carolyn Grace Imgruet.

IT COULDN'T HAVE been a more beautiful early summer day in 1969. I'd graduated from Bloom High School the year before and had been attending Prairie State Junior College, known to many as the Columbia of the Midwest.

Okay, not anyone with a functioning brain thinks that, but it sounds good.

My parents didn't really have the money for a four-year school at that point and I didn't really care. I did have the '69 Dodge Charger R/T, but there was no way I—or my parents—had any desire to face the burden of a ton of college debt.

Besides, I had no set idea what I wanted to do with my life, even if the journalism thing seemed to be my best bet. So why not just get my general education requirements out of the way at Prairie State and see where I was in a couple of years.

More importantly, why not just drive the fuck out of that car and not be all that challenged by school stuff. There was also this little matter of the war in Vietnam, which at the time was raging on with no end in sight.

It's not that I wouldn't have served my country as my dad had done, it's just that I hated that war because I knew it was wrong.

But I digress.

Anyway, the temperature was pushing 90 degrees that day. There wasn't a cloud in the sky and I was starting a new job at the Jack-in-the-Box on Joe Orr Road in Chicago Heights.

And yes, there actually used to be a Jack there.

On this particular day, franchise owner Armando Cruz, who holds the unique distinction of being the only boss who ever fired me, decided that the curbs all around the place needed painting.

Next thing I knew, I was outside with a can of yellow paint along with fellow employee Jim Dunn, a guy who'd grown up just a couple of blocks from me.

The thing you have to understand about Dunn is that he was my polar opposite.

For as long as I'd known him he was like every guy who's earned his reputation as a Lady Killer. A veteran of the dating wars with plenty of scalps to prove it. He almost claimed to be the best pure shooter in Illinois when we played basketball. And in case you didn't believe he was the most handsome man alive, all you had to do was ask him.

Me? Not so much.

Little did I know that very day we were both being sized up by Carolyn and Barb Taylor, yet another of my ex-Bloom classmates, both of whom had arrived for work after we'd been manning the curbs for a while.

I later found out that Carolyn asked for dibs on me, Taylor chose Dunn.

Yeah, I was quite a catch all right.

I have no doubt I was covered in yellow paint (sadly, I paint the way a tapir shits), probably overweight, and it's possible I smelled bad because it was getting warmer as that morning rolled into afternoon.

The even bigger picture was that I had no real direction in life, no money, and seemingly no hopes of ever getting any. I drove way too fast and my best friend at the time, Bob Aebi, was a 6'5" 280-pound whack job whose sole interest in life was preparing to become a professional wrestler.

The fact that Carolyn and I soon became an item had to be every bit as big an upset as Joe Namath's Jets pulled off by beating the Colts in Super Bowl III.

To say I was a complete novice in the whole dating thing would be an understatement, given the fact that I'd gotten through the four sometimes tortuous years of high school without a single steady girl.

Thing is that was okay. I didn't waste a moment worrying about it. Sure, there were a few girls around who I was attracted to, but that never translated into me actually saying anything to them. I don't know if girls found me funny or pathetic. Maybe both.

Carolyn and I at Homewood-Flossmoor High School's prom in 1970.

HERE'S WHAT I knew for sure early on—I was in love.

So how do you know you're in love if you've never before been in love?

You just do.

Sorry, that's the best I got.

If you need deeper meaning, tune in Dr. Phil, whose TV show is just a half-step ahead of the old Jerry Springer fuck fest on the stupid meter.

But believe me there were obstacles.

While my parents absolutely loved Carolyn, her mom didn't much get my whole act.

In retrospect, I can't say that I blame her.

I didn't drive any slower, I didn't stop my late-night gambling forays to the old Sportsman's Park, and I couldn't offer a single notion as to what I might be doing in five years. Hell, make that five minutes.

Given the premise that few mothers like the guys who come around to date their daughters anyway, I was batting .000 before I ever got in the door.

No wonder she made a habit of throwing me out of the house on Constance Lane in Chicago Heights, sometimes with gentle prodding, other times with far less subtlety. And always right around 9 PM.

Lucky for me, I was nothing if not persistent.

I made an appearance at her house every night, somehow managing to rile up just about everybody at one time or another, although her dad, Joe, was always cool with me.

With two brothers, Joe and Bill, and three sisters, Janet, Mary, and Cathy, I was suddenly in the middle of something I'd never experienced as an only child.

So how hard did I have to work to get at least the majority of them to like me?

I knew that Cathy, the youngest sibling, wasn't coming over to my side anytime soon. That was okay, she was 6 or 7 at the time and took tremendous joy in making my life miserable and getting away with it. Besides, she was Mommy's little narc, sent outside solely to see what was going on. And making my life miserable in the process.

The positive here is that over a period of time I worked my way onto the good side of Carol's siblings, or at least good enough, if you count beating their ass on the driveway basketball court. That was no great shakes. Her brothers were roughly 3 feet tall, so I was hardly reinventing basketball moves to get the best of them and their friends, who I should mention were also about 3 feet tall and not rising.

BESIDES THE EXHILARATING feeling of being in love for the first time, there was another hidden bonus in the relationship—it kept me out of Steger for several hours a day.

Why is that a big deal?

Because the Steger cops treated me as I were running a goddamn Colombian drug cartel.

How would anyone like it if they were being stopped an average of four times a week the minute just they got inside the city limits?

They'd put the mars lights on so often I was getting a tan. They'd pull me over and claim that several people had complained that I had been speeding through the streets, creating a nuisance and leaving in my wake folks frightened for their very existence.

My reply was simple. How exactly was I speeding around my neighborhood streets if I hadn't even been there?

The answer from the police was always the same. People heard your car tearing up the streets and they were sick of it. The complaints were stacking up and it was the guy in the red Charger.

No, it fucking wasn't.

I finally gave up trying to explain to them that I wasn't around, but I did make note that there were other cars that sounded exactly like mine in the neighborhood, including a Plymouth Road Runner and a Super Bee.

Since both were driven by friends of mine, I withheld all other information. Yeah, I know, they could have figured it out easily enough had they been willing to put forth a bit more effort. They never did. The bullseye remained squarely trained on me, even though I could have added the word rat bastard to my résumé for blaming my buddies.

Now don't get me wrong. As you already know, I'm a born speeder and I love fast cars. It just wasn't happening the way they claimed. And yes, while I've acquired a few speeding tickets over the years, none of them came courtesy of the Steger cops.

The one ticket I almost got was for allegedly driving around a barricade in a school zone, going down a rather steep grass hill in the process. That never happened. No matter, it brought Officer Charles Tieri to my door, much to my parents' consternation, especially my mom, who hated the thought of the neighbors seeing a squad car out front. Of course, she also hated many of our neighbors, especially the old cock spank next door.

I don't know if I'd ever thought that much about men's cologne before that charming night, but Tieri, or Porky as folks called him, must have been soaking in it. I swear that for a week after he left I could still smell his scent in the house. Good thing he didn't have another officer with him, or we would have really gotten our two scents worth.

His claim that my car had been identified as the offending party was a load of shit. First of all, I hadn't been near that school in years, and second, there's no way I was driving that Charger up and down any steep grassy hills, no matter how bad a driver I was.

Some quarter miles, yes, but never in Steger. And I was never a fool on a hill.

Despite his inability to provide anything remotely resembling proof that I had done it, Tieri insisted there was enough evidence to give me what would have been a very expensive ticket.

Carolyn's family—(from left) parents Rita and Joe and sisters Cathy and Mary—loved the car, not so much the driver.

Ultimately, he didn't, issuing me yet another stern warning that if I kept driving in such a reckless fashion, my day was coming and I was not going to like it one bit.

Fuck him and the horse he rode in on.

My mother, of course, was fuming after Perfumania left the house. I hoped she was just briefly overcome by the cologne, but no such luck. "I don't believe you did that," she said. "But I know you've done something. I can't take it anymore."

And what is it I've done, I asked, as if I didn't know.

"You drive way too fast and you're not all that good of a driver," she said. "You know it, I know it, and your dad knows it. Keep this up and we're going to take away the car. I mean it. You're going to kill yourself, or somebody else."

That wasn't the first time I'd heard that. So I agreed. I just didn't want to fight a war on so many fronts, especially since I knew she was right. I wasn't the kind of kid who would drive into a ditch to get around a parking barricade, but I wasn't very good behind the wheel, although I got plenty of places in a hurry.

But even then, I still blamed Porky for coming to our house for what amounted to a fishing expedition, unable to provide a shred of proof for his baseless accusation.

Only years later, long after I stopped thinking about him, did I see an item on the TV news that did my heart good.

While Porky was still the chief, someone held up the K-Mart in town that was built long after I was gone. The Steger police and others had marshaled their forces that day and surrounded the building, believing the robber was still inside, that they had their man cornered.

After 10 hours of waiting, the cops finally moved in, ready to end the supposed standoff, arrest the perp, and give him a taste of Hai Karate.

Of course, the bad guy had been gone for hours. I seem to recall he was found the next day in Tennessee.

And that, at least to me, proved the ancient Boers proverb: Once a numb nuts, always a numb nuts.

chapter 10

Murph

During my 25 years at The Score, I believe it's quite possible that I was a part of as many remote broadcasts as anyone who's ever had a radio show.

And while I generally would prefer not to play fast and loose with the facts, we're probably looking at a figure of somewhere around 500-plus shows on the road. Some were close to home, others not so close. And that includes several Super Bowls, a few NBA championship runs with the Bulls, a trip to Houston for the 2005 World Series between the White Sox and Astros, as well as the Miami trip in 2003 for the Cubs-Marlins NLCS. My last trip was Super Bowl L in San Francisco, just for old time's sake.

Those road trips were all sweet rewards, not just because we put ourselves in the center of the action and helped forward our brand, but also because I don't recall ever not being asked the question most people have wanted to know since the station began, namely, "What's up between you and [Mike] Murphy?"

In the interest of brevity for a topic that grew old in a hurry, I would usually refer to Murph as a certain body part. There are only two real good choices. Pick either. I've probably used those two and others over the years.

But here's something most people don't know—my wife and I were actually at Murph's wedding reception, which, of course, was at Wrigley Field.

Here's the only detail I recall. I was in line to get food when Ron Santo sidled up to me. "Hey," Santo said. "I just wanted you to know that you're an asshole." Santo paused a moment, then added, "You know what you're talking about, but you're still an asshole."

My clever rejoinder, "Okay." By that time Santo had walked away, never to say another word to me. I tried to think if we'd ever exchanged greetings of any kind over the years when I'd been with the *Sun-Times*, but came up empty. Kind of amazing, really, but our paths had never crossed, not even in the press box. But then again, maybe Santo's take on me was made strictly through the early days of The Score. I'm not sure that was possible, but I'll never know.

I took no offense, really. If that's the worst thing someone has called me then I'm way ahead of the game, right Diana Ditka? I did find it puzzling that he chose that particular moment to vent whatever frustration had been building, but since I never saw him again in person, it was the only chance he would get.

Over time, I've come to realize it was all rather inconsequential. I never lost a moment's sleep over Santo hating me, and not much more time would pass before Murphy came around to that same way of thinking.

Thing is, Murphy built his early animus based on a completely false premise. Another shocker, eh? Or haven't you heard his show?

I can trace the earliest seeds of the feud back to the old bunker on Belmont. McNeil and I were cutting a spot for one of the restaurants that would eventually go out of business (we were quite good at that, maybe the best ever) and Murph was in the booth in front of us in a gaudy leather outfit that caught our attention, especially mine.

Aren't clothes worn to be made fun of?

Sure, they are. Especially leather pants. Just a character flaw of mine, I guess. It takes a village, people.

But Murph noticed. I couldn't stop laughing. You'd think that a guy who was a Cubs Bleacher Bum back in the '60s would have a better sense of humor. He didn't. Was that the genesis of the bad blood? I'd have to say so because he suddenly broke out in this bizarre little double bird pumping frenzy, which to this day makes production genius Russ Mitera chuckle. He had no idea what Murph's problem was that or any other day, but he readily confesses to enjoying the moment immensely.

Who doesn't? Thing is, no matter what the actual truth was, it never got in the way of Murph's anger towards me. What makes it all even better is that practically every bit of the hatred for me was completely misdirected.

Let me explain. Back in the early days of the Wild, Wild Score, we were basically allowed to have some fun (or not) at the expense of another host. Such shenanigans would later become taboo, but by that time several feathers had been ruffled, none more so than those of Murphy, Chicago's very own Leatherman.

Because he didn't know jack shit about much of anything apart from his beloved Cubs, Murphy was prone to pronounce names wrong, get some facts screwed up, and in general have some flights of fancy, including the one cut he played about the

Cubs "soaping up and singing in the shower" that we couldn't get enough of.

The names he butchered included Dallas Cowboys coach Barry Switzer, who mysteriously became "Coach Schweitzer" on the evening show. There were others, but you get the picture.

And whose fault was it that those drops became a staple of the afternoon show? Mine, of course.

I actually stood accused of going back through his shows and cutting the tape, at least in Murphy's skewed sense of reality.

I couldn't have done that if my life depended on it. I'd worked at newspapers for 20 years, never studied anything radio in my life, and knew zilch about the process of cutting up tape. I didn't even know if that was the right term. I'm not saying I didn't love the results, but my hands were clean. And one other thing, I didn't listen to his show, so I had no idea of what he did or didn't do, unless someone else tried to fill me in.

And if you're thinking that I must have put someone on Murph's trail, I did not. To make someone listen could well have been an enormous abuse of power.

But despite all of this, I discovered that innocence is not a defense in the insipid world of Judge Murph.

And Murphy did all of this knowing that McNeil was the true radio guy and Judd Sirott never missed a trick when it came to the evening show. If Murph said something silly, missed a name, or just sounded like a braying ass, we would have it. And you know who else would drop a Murph goodie on us whenever he could? Russ Mitera. I didn't even know that until Russ hit me with that tidbit while we were having lunch last May. That's how out of touch I was with the entire process.

I'll say this for Murphy, he certainly could hold a grudge. Well after his nonsense ceased being played, he continued to be prickly. This from the guy who would handwrite as many as 17 pages (with minimal spacing) of notes concerning station problems on a legal pad and hand them to onetime general manager Harvey Wells. I don't know why, but Harvey once told me he read every page. Poor bastard. I knew he was Murph's friend, but actually talking to him seemed to be far too high a price to pay, let alone suffering through 17 pages of his bullshit.

I was ultimately hoping that Murphy would just drift into the gloamin' or that we would find someone else to host who wasn't a five-alarm ass wipe. Is that too much to ask?

Apparently, it was for far too long a time.

After the in-house turmoil of the station in 1999 and the odd schedule shifts that came with it, we actually began to see more of Murphy, particularly after shifting our base of operation to the NBC Tower.

What a terrible break that was for me and Bernstein, whose opinion of Murphy was no different than mine. Truthfully, it would have been ultra-difficult to find anyone who did like him, with the exception of his onetime partner Fred Huebner. There was just nothing about him to like, no matter how hard you tried to find a reason.

And because we now had more office space at NBC, Murphy's many quirks were on full display.

Here's a small sample size. Whenever he went to the bathroom at the Tower, he would immediately flush all the toilets so he couldn't hear any of our show, which was being piped into the restroom.

He would also walk well out of his way just to make sure he didn't cross my path, although no threats had ever been exchanged, unless you count the double finger from years ago. Then came my personal favorite.

On one of the days I was working from home, Murphy actually had gone into our studio with Bernstein. Uncomfortable? Oh, yeah. Bernstein learned that Murph apparently wanted to talk to me about something, God only knows what. Finally, Dan told him that I wasn't coming in that day. Without saying a word, he got up from his chair in the corner and left the studio.

Turns out it couldn't have been all that important because on the days I was in the office after that, he never approached me, never said a thing to me, and still did his best to avoid me.

Let the record show that when he did his last Score show on June 12, 2009, there was no one around who expressed the least bit of regret. No one was sorry and I've never heard a single soul say they miss him.

That didn't surprise anyone.

While I might have been the main target of his anger, I had nothing to do with the fact that two of his producers hated him so much they actually planned to jump him in the parking lot and beat him with a sack full of quarters, simply because he was such a dick. I'm glad they didn't. I like both of them very much and would have hated to see them get in trouble for doing something so foolish.

Here's what Murph should be worried about: His own temper.

I remember walking into a Wrigleyville bar one day several years back to do our show and being immediately told of a temper tantrum he'd just thrown. I think it was over one of his idiotic 3 second sound drops. Or maybe it was one of his idiotic 7 second soundbites. He'd completely lost it in the bar, throwing stuff around in his fit of pique.

I've seen a lot of people get mad over a lot of things, but this was about as insignificant as it could possibly be. It's doubtful that anyone listening would have even noticed there was a problem. It was just business as usual.

So, no, I don't mind staying on the wrong side of Murphy, especially when you consider there is no right side.

I suppose I've acquired any number of enemies over my years in the media. It's just part of the gig, no matter if it was newspapers or radio or TV. I'm sure that if there had been Twitter back in the days when I wrote a column, I would have been bashed and battered more than once by an angry populace. That's part of the deal, although I'm not sure anyone could have been any angrier than the PETA woman from St. Charles who sent me letters (yes, actual snail mail) for six months after I wrote a column about eating dog during my stay in Seoul for the '88 Olympics.

She actually amused me with her own unique brand of vitriol.

Murph? Not so much. He's just the type of guy you hope that you never wind up sitting next to on a plane. Or, for that matter, anyplace else.

At least now if he's mad, I get it. Not that most people who are fans of The Score haven't known it for a long, long time. But I know you can't make Murph miserable. He has been for decades.

chapter 11

John

After Carolyn and I had been dating for about six months, my mom did something completely out of character, at least for her. She basically asked me what's up with this sudden girl thing. I remember I wasn't sure how to reply. It was something she'd never had to ask before. Or, for that matter, ever needed to ask again.

Caught completely off guard for a second, I decided to play dumb, something I had a lot of practice at. "In regards to," I said, hitting the pause button.

"Well," she said. "I really like Carolyn and your dad does, too. We were just wondering if there's anything going on we should know about."

I chose to be honest with her, something I hadn't always been over the years. I told her that Carolyn and I had indeed been talking about getting engaged before I packed up and headed to Northern Illinois in the fall, although nothing was official yet.

That seemed to make her happy, although I knew that finishing my education remained foremost in her mind. Same for me. If I was going to make a go of this journalism thing, getting my degree was the only road available.

As things turned out, the suspense didn't last all that much longer.

By the time we reached the early stages of 1971, things changed drastically, and most unexpectedly. I'd been coming home every weekend in the Charger, but I told her that driving the thing in winter months was hardly fun, that it was possible I could miss a weekend or two here and there.

It was just the winter before when I got stuck in the middle of a street because the two back tires were on patches of ice. Luckily, that had happened right in front of my house so I had all the help I needed. Talk about spinning your wheels.

What I learned in January was far more surprising—Carolyn was pregnant.

Maybe surprising isn't the right word, but you know what I'm saying. We went from young and in love to planning a wedding. Well, not so much me. Because I'd never spent a minute of my life even thinking about such things, all I could hope was that she wouldn't be disappointed that this wouldn't be the storybook wedding that many women dream about.

And it wasn't. It didn't take much planning to come up with this one. We would be married at St. Liborius Church in Steger, where the word lavish has never, ever even been used.

I would be able to have the people in my family who really cared on hand plus three friends, including Downey. She would have none of her friends present (still a sore point with her), but then she did have a much larger family, including many more aunts and uncles, some of whom I'm not sure I ever saw sober. They knew how to party.

The reception would be at her house in Chicago Heights, where I kind of figured I might still need an official taster, because her mom and I had never completely worked things out from the rough beginning. That would still take a few more years to accomplish.

The date was Feb. 20, 1971. It was first major step in what would turn out to be my sometimes painful process of growing up. The second step would come in August of that year when our oldest son, John, was born.

And for the record, our honeymoon night was spent at a motel in Homewood. Hey, it's the best we could do. Actually, we never managed to get away until the summer of '74 when we made a trip to San Francisco and then drove down the Pacific Coast Highway to Los Angeles where we stayed in Hollywood. Was it ultimately worth the wait? Yep, we had a blast.

DESPITE HAVING BEEN in two businesses that are known to produce some folks with massive egos, I spent a great deal of my adult life thinking of myself as a chronic underachiever.

I saw myself as a guy who'd skated for too much of his life without ever fulfilling a bit of the promise my parents had once seen, a guy who might have been able to do great things with his life if he'd only cared a little bit more.

Sorry if that sounds presumptuous. It's not meant to be. I honestly felt that way, even if I wasn't exactly known for being quite so introspective or, for that matter, the least bit thoughtful.

I had waltzed through Bloom High School without leaving a single mark and barely opening a book, had done the same in college until my final year at Northern Illinois when I realized that if I didn't start acting like the studies were important to me, no one was going to hire a middle-of-the-class journalism imbecile, although being an imbecile in the early '70s was hardly a rarity.

Lucky for me that someone at the Sun-Journal Newspapers saw more than that, giving me that first job in June in '72, fresh out of Northern Illinois' journalism school.

I mention this only because I was just about to turn 45 years old before I finally started to feel comfortable in my own skin.

CAROL AND I were walking the along the beachfront in Lake Geneva, Wisconsin during a typically warm August evening when I suddenly stopped and sat on one of the benches.

I felt myself being overcome by this sudden wave of emotion.

Maybe it was because I was finally comfortable with the radio thing or maybe it was because I knew there was a new contract on the way that would hopefully put me in uncharted earnings territory or maybe it was because I'd finally realized something I'd known all along.

"You feeling okay?" Carol asked.

"I don't think I've ever been better," was my answer, coming to immediate grips with what was happening.

I've always been prone to beating myself up over my career, second-guessing myself like crazy, somehow managing to dwell on the mistakes rather than the good times. That night, with that bolt from the starlit Wisconsin sky, I was suddenly able to like myself, at least more than I had in years.

At last I could finally stop and allow myself the luxury of feeling good.

Even though I'd never doubted the most important job anyone has in their life is raising their kids, it's easy to forget that at times.

I mean if you're going to spend so much time obsessing over what could have been or the day-to-day grind that can wear anyone down, why not spend some time thinking about the positives?

My oldest son, John, turned into just what we always thought he would be: a really wonderful adult with a great moral compass.

Our second oldest, Joe, was just hitting his stride after graduating from Lincoln-Way, pursuing his baseball career at Joliet Junior College and leaving no doubt that he would one day seek a career in law enforcement.

Our youngest, twins Chris and Cary, were about to turn 12, and we were as convinced as any parents can be that both would someday make their way in the world just fine.

I had tears in my eyes that night, even if I'd never been happier.

I'd told Carol for years that she'd done a great job raising our sons because I'd been on the road so much for the *Sun-Times* between 1982 and '92, not to mention being little more than a weekend visitor to home for about the first six months I worked at the *Detroit Free Press* starting in 1978.

She understood that. She also knew that if you're going to be covering the Bulls and eventually writing a column it all goes with the territory. But there will always be regrets.

And apparently there will always be tears.

There are an increasing number of things that bring tears to my eyes these days. I don't know if it's a function of getting older or maybe even getting crazier, but I tear up quite frequently. I'm not the emotional wreck I once was, but my sensitivity to things has definitely increased.

I also realize that when it comes to the kids, we've been pretty fortunate, especially after going through what turned out to be the some of the most traumatic moments any parents can experience.

JOHN WAS SIX years old when he was diagnosed with acute lymphocytic leukemia. Just hearing those words shook me to the core. He was one very sick little boy and I don't care how strong a person you think you are, there's nothing that prepares you for what's ahead.

His condition was such that he was sent by ambulance from St. James Hospital in Chicago Heights to the old Children's

My dad (left), John, and Emil at Christmas at Grandma's house in 1972.

Memorial Hospital in the city. It was all happening so fast. I'd lost my mom in 1972, my dad in '74, and I was now coping with the reality of yet another life and death struggle.

I remember little about that first trip down to Children's. Maybe my mind has completely blocked out the details after all these years. But I'm not complaining.

We were both scared and deeply shaken, entering into uncharted waters and struggling to fully comprehend what lie ahead for our beautiful six-year-old son.

Enter Dr. Elaine Morgan, the woman who would ultimately save John's life.

Some background. We were told that despite her relative youth, Dr. Morgan was one of the best children's oncologists in the country, that she was thorough and determined, that we couldn't be in better hands.

She laid out the treatment plan for John the first time we sat with her, noting that the decision on whether or not he needed radiation treatments would be determined at a later date.

She also gave John a 60 percent chance for a full recovery, odds that would be pleasing to most. But even as I put my supposed brave front forward, I felt as if all the air had been knocked out of me.

Realizing that being a simpering mass of gooey flesh wasn't going to help anyone, particularly Carol, I took the news like an adult.

But I cried myself to sleep that night. And the next night. And the next. I kept that to myself, but I think she knew it. But you absolutely can't let the negative thoughts take over your life.

Thankfully, within a relatively short amount of time, Dr. Morgan told us that John's leukemia was in full remission, that all signs remained very much positive and that his prognosis remained good.

But the worst was yet to come.

WE KNEW THAT the one thing John couldn't get was chicken pox. Dr. Morgan had warned us from the beginning if that happened, all cards were off the table.

And sure enough he got chicken pox, creating a crisis that lasted for more than a week and left John, who was already on life support, teetering on the edge of life and death after his breathing apparatus was somehow unplugged.

While we had slept some of the time at the Ronald McDonald House, this would be the week of hallway couches, soul-searching, and the power of prayers that we both shared for what was probably the first time.

Finally, on Day 4, when we were both exhausted, when the mental drain had taken just about everything out of us, word came that John would survive the crisis, that he was at last breathing on his own.

We hugged each other and cried. I don't know that you can adequately describe what that moment was like. I knew I had run out of words. My emotions were all over the map.

John would eventually be allowed to go home a few days later, but his treatments continued and ultimately there was no additional chemo.

And while John would at times be willing to go back to Children's for the meetings with other cancer survivors, he didn't

John's three children (left to right) Delaney, Ellie, and Connor.

really like to do it. His preference was to never go back again—and that was fine with us.

It wasn't until Jan. 26, 2010, which happened to mark the 36th year after my dad's passing, that we finally sent the following email to Dr. Morgan.

> Dear Dr. Morgan,
>
> I don't know if you'll remember us, but you treated our son, John, for leukemia back in the late 1970s.
>
> We think about you often, but we've been remiss in not sending a line before now, and for that, we apologize.
>
> Sometimes life just gets in the way of the things you really ought to do, such as acknowledging those to whom you're forever indebted.
>
> And while it isn't as if our memory needed jogging, we both caught you the other night on the Channel 2 News at 10 with the two Haitian kids who are the newest members of your family.
>
> Congratulations on that, but to those of us who've known you even in times of extreme stress, your actions are hardly surprising.
>
> We understand that brings your total to six kids now, so we've enclosed pictures of John's three kids, who are the lights of our life as are our two other grandchildren.
>
> John, who turned 38 in August, is doing quite well for himself these days in the business world, as are his three male siblings.
>
> My wife said how great you looked on TV, and then both had a good laugh when we remembered that you

were only about three years older than I was when we brought John to you.

Here's what I know.

I was 26 when John was diagnosed and Carol was 24. We thought our world was ending.

You not only gave us hope on some of the darkest days—I can still hear John screaming when he used to get the spinal tap—but you always treated him with a genuine affection that we will never, ever forget.

It may seem trite to simply say thank you again, but I'll say it on the behalf of two proud parents and a ton of other people who've come to know our oldest son over the years.

We understand our debt of gratitude to you cannot possibly be repaid in words, but I think it's OK when the words are long overdue.

Sincerely,
Carol and Terry Boers

I'M GUESSING THAT Dr. Morgan has received countless letters from grateful parents over the years. And I'd bet she's answered each and every one of them. We heard back the next day, and she mentioned how beautiful the kids were, and yes, she said still vividly remembered John.

I have no idea why all of that hit me that long ago night in Lake Geneva. It was as if I had hit some kind of rewind button and the images were there, flipping through my life, perhaps even allowing me to at least cut myself a little slack, something I've seldom done.

Little did I know what the next 20 or so years would bring, how my life would change again, including the breakup of The Heavy Fuel Crew, the births of five grandchildren and the continued rise of The Score in both popularity and revenue. And there would even be baseball on the station, starting with the World Champion Chicago White Sox.

But there would be trying personal times, too. You might be able to run from some things, but life always catches up with you, often at the worst possible times. I've always been cautioned not to let the tough times outweigh the good, that it's best to just keep your head up even if your heart is breaking. I suppose that makes perfect sense. Thing is, sometimes you just get really tired of being tested. More about that later.

chapter 12

Trouble

As The Score passed its seven-year birth milestone, I promise you that no one in management or on the air was partying like it was 1999.

The ratings had never quite bounced back following the switch to the shitty 1160 frequency, which had remained a nagging problem to us and the listeners, at least to those who hadn't already abandoned ship.

While it was impossible to calculate exactly how much damage had been done on that front, there were other things happening that were even trickier, even worse for the station's long term health.

Put succinctly, the little station that thought it could had become a place where pettiness and jealousy had moved from the backburner to center stage.

That made us, I suppose, not unlike many radio stations or other workplaces in general. But that wasn't what we were supposed to be about.

"It has to be about the entertainment," Gleason once told me. "People come here to get away from their problems."

Good advice. But sometimes the hurt feelings and bruised egos amongst the hosts were far more noticeable. Too many of our trademark transitions with the Monsters had devolved into pissing sessions, both on a personal and business level. And yes, the war with Murphy also fell into that category.

While Danny and I never transitioned with him, some deemed our actions as childish and unnecessary on a professional level. We thought quite the opposite, believing he deserved everything he got and then some.

There was also the matter of money. The word in the hallways was that North had been given a huge deal that dwarfed everyone else, something in the neighborhood of $500,000 to $600,000 per year. A few years later, after going on a pilgrimage to Landover, Maryland, to meet with company President and CEO Dan Mason, that number would increase dramatically.

No one was sure exactly how much North's kitty grew, but some insisted he had crossed the great Potomac that day and was well into seven figures per year.

I don't think Danny or I fell into that money trap. I liked the idea that the money was there, that it was something to shoot for in the years ahead. And no, I never came close to it, and I know Danny didn't either. So was it all about the money or not?

Gleason insisted at the time that most of the friction stemmed from the never-ending quest for good guests, that every show wanted the very best, and the very best were being spread thinner and thinner with sports talk hitting a boom phase around the country.

Again, Danny and I didn't look at it quite that way. Did we love good guests? Sure, guys like Doug Collins, Matt Millen, Mike Bauman from Milwaukee, Norman Chad, Todd Christensen, and Danny Plesac were prime examples. All of them were great, all were willing participants in whatever nonsense we were up to that day. And for that, we owe them a deep debt of gratitude for their time.

All of them—and others—were in sharp contrast to some of the guys the station paid. If you ever heard one of the Monday sessions with former Bears defensive coordinator and Eagles head coach Buddy Ryan, you know what I mean.

Getting him on the air from his horse farm in Kentucky, Ryan was probably the only football expert of his day who didn't seem to know who Steelers running back Barry Foster was. That, however, was just the proverbial tip of the iceberg. What became clearer and clearer as time rolled on was that Ryan didn't watch any of the weekend NFL games.

It was great to command all the love that Buddy got from grateful Bears fans, but a little more insight might have helped. Actually, any insight would have helped. But when in doubt, you could always talk about the '85 Bears.

Luckily, at least from my point of view, I always felt that while great guests are a tasty radio cookie, ultimately the responsibility to entertain falls on the hosts. There just aren't any awards given to producers with great rolodexes, although there probably should be.

In my world, there are no radio scapegoats. Your failure is your failure. It's not because of this or that, it's because at the end of the day you sucked. Your name was on it. You're the one who was bad. Not once in my 25 years did I single out any of the brilliant executive producers I've worked with over the years and hold them accountable for a bad show. And there were plenty of bad ones, even as Danny and I somehow managed to hold serve, despite the problems.

The station, meanwhile, had already undergone some changes. Tom Shaer, who'd been teamed for some of the time with Jim Memolo in the mornings, failed to reach a contract agreement in 1997 and left the station.

In his place were "The Bull and the Bear," Norm Van Lier and the great Doug Buffone.

I had the feeling from the very beginning that this show was doomed to fail. I loved both of them dearly, especially Doug, whose signature rants after Bears games had made him a station legend, along with another former outspoken Bear, Ed O'Bradovich. But the morning thing was a disaster, just as I feared it would be. Neither one of them seemed particularly comfortable being the lead dog, so the direction of the show, at least on most days, was in the drifting position, as in man, that's a tough listen.

That bothered me. I certainly didn't want them to suck, but it became clear early on that there was just no getting around it. Although both were colorful guys full of great stories, the show never got off the ground in a market with some terrific morning shows.

And little did I know that our day of reckoning was coming, too.

THE DATE WAS July 16, 1999. Carolyn and I were hosting a party for Score people at our old house in Mokena. And if you're wondering how I remember it so vividly, that was the day John F. Kennedy Jr. died after crashing his airplane into the Atlantic Ocean just off the coast of Martha's Vineyard.

I recall that as people came in, we were all gathered around the living room TV watching when the word became official that JFK Jr. had perished. The official ruling would be that he had fallen victim to spatial disorientation while over the water. That led to him losing control of the aircraft.

A sobering moment, indeed. But we recovered enough to have fun and the usual laughs. Then, after most people had gone home, Mike North and I were sitting around the kitchen table shooting the breeze.

Then, out of the blue, North asked me what would I think about working from 8 to noon, hours that I'd never heard before in terms of radio.

"Not sure," I finally answered. "I'd have to get up pretty damn early to get down to Belmont Ave. Why do you ask?"

"Just wondering," North said, adding nothing more.

I don't think I was overly concerned. It sounded like one of those silly questions that sometimes gets asked. But it did nag me for a bit. A little more than a month later, I got an urgent call to get in early, that Wells and Gleason wanted to see me. No hint was offered as to what the meeting was about.

But I had this bad feeling in the pit of my stomach as I made my way to Belmont Ave. The news was abrupt and to the point. Danny and I were done as a team. And just like that, 7½ fun years were down the drain, meaning that ultimately, at least in my mind, The Heavy Fuel Crew had crashed and burned.

They emphasized to me that that wasn't the case, that it was just something they felt necessary to freshen up the station. The ratings had been "soft." And, yes, the hours had been shifted around to that odd configuration North had spoken of the previous month, getting far away from the hours radio listeners had become accustomed to.

North and Jiggetts were also kaput. North would work mornings by himself, I would be teamed with Score reporter Dan Bernstein in the 8-12 slot and Danny had landed with Jiggetts in the 4-8 deathtrap.

Let the uproar begin.

If I had to handicap the field on sheer anger, Danny would have been the man. He flat out had no desire to work with Jiggetts. And, believe or not, it wasn't personal. He liked Dan. He just didn't want to work with him, especially not in those awful hours. Even when you say that, it sounds stupid. But to the best of my knowledge, I know that's correct.

For his part, Wells, sensing some fraying around the edges of the shows and relationships, didn't really care. He wanted done what he wanted done and that was it. Period. Paragraph. There was no room for bargaining here. No way to get even the slightest leverage. The ratings weren't awful, but the numbers more or less backed up his argument.

More importantly, he thought he was right.

That many of us disagreed mattered not. When you're running a radio station, that's what you want—autonomy. Harvey had it, wielded it, and felt confident he'd done the right thing.

But had he? History suggests he wasn't all wrong, but he'd swung and missed on two of the three shows that were created that day. And I mean swung and missed big time. He was only right about one show, and I'm betting you know which one.

When Bernstein and I had our first informal meeting in the bloody aftermath, we simply stepped out the back door of the old Belmont Ave. bunker with Gleason for a private chat.

Few would have guessed when I was paired up with Dan in 1999 that Boers and Bernstein would become the standard bearer for the station. *(Courtesy of 670 The Score)*

Although people at the station were well aware of Gleason's love for Bernstein, the first words out of his mouth to us that day were, "This is Terry's show."

I stopped him right there. I'm not a programmer, but I certainly didn't feel that was what I wanted. "This is our show," I interjected. "I'm not the star of anything. We're going to succeed or fail because of what we do, not what I do."

And I did it without a hint of false modesty. My seven-plus years of investment in the station were real enough, but I was unable to ascertain if people liked me, or if I was just riding along with those who loved Danny going back to his Coppock days.

Whether that was true or false, I'll never be able to answer. It just strikes me that the best partnerships are the ones shared equally, not much different from marriage in most ways.

I talked about chemistry earlier. I knew Danny Mac and I had enough of it. Would it be the same with Bernstein, who was a completely different type of guy?

No way to be sure unless you do it. I can tell you this, I'd put a lot of time and energy into this whole thing, and it was way, way too late to decide on another career shift. I'd grown to liking the medium more than I ever thought I would, but now all my remaining chips were on the table and I sensed I'd lost more than a few of them.

If Harvey and Ron had wanted to get me out of my comfort zone, they'd more than succeeded.

I felt a lot uncertainty in those days, even letting more than a little doubt creep into the mix, something that hadn't happened in years. Everything I'd done professionally I had eventually nailed, including working on a sports desk at two major metropolitan dailies, covering a beat, and writing a column.

There was a steep learning curve to those jobs. You often had just fleeing moments to edit on deadline and at times just minutes to write on deadline. You had to be alert and ultra-organized. Most of all, you had to be prepared to listen.

So here I was again, at another career crossroads, fully comprehending that failure to launch wasn't going to be acceptable.

I had two sons who would soon be readying for college, plus there were plenty of other bills that were more important than a 4:30 AM wakeup call.

We were down to the last Boers' radio stand, and this was strictly a pass-fail proposition. I could still remember my high school days when getting a C on my report card was a huge relief. Not to my mother, maybe, but it was to me.

Boers and Bernstein couldn't just be acceptable to a far more discerning audience. Rough patches might have been expected and even allowed, but the final product couldn't be anything but great.

Yes, I'd ordered a tall one for myself, but that's what I wanted. You might not clear the bar every time you jump, but I don't think anyone does. We just had to find a style, a way to do things that would establish a strong identity for both of us, something that seems easy enough, but can be hard as hell.

So with my 49th birthday approaching, I was a combination of angst and energy, ready to get this thing started in grand fashion, as if my life depended on it. And guess what? In many ways it did.

chapter 13

John E.

What did it mean in September 1974 when I left the *Lansing Sun-Journal* for the *Chicago Heights Star*?

Everything. And I'm not even including the $50 a week pay increase I was going to get. You see, unless you were raised in the south suburbs roughly 40 to 50 years ago, the name John E. Meyers probably doesn't jog your memory.

For the record, he was the sports editor of the *Chicago Heights Star* for more than 50 years before retiring in 1984 as the executive sports editor of all the *Star-Tribune* newspapers.

Most of all, he was known for his twice-a-week column, The Hot Corner. That name probably sounds pretty damn corny to many today. It probably brings to mind some ridiculous old coot root, root, rooting for the high school home team and moaning when they didn't win. That assumption would be terribly incorrect.

He was the *Chicago Heights Star*. And you can use the S in star either in upper or lower case. John was both.

He covered every sports issue of the day and he did it beautifully. Same goes for social issues. John never held back.

I was probably about 15 when The Hot Corner first caught my eye, only because I had an English teacher at Bloom High School recommend it to me, saying that if I was truly serious about writing for a newspaper, read John.

Actually, I wasn't truly serious about much of anything back then, but I did what she asked. And I immediately loved it.

I had no idea then that my tiny connection to John would someday lead to the greatest five years I would have ever have in my 20-year newspaper career.

That will take a little explaining, so let's start with the awful day of Saturday, Jan. 26, 1974. Richard Nixon was president and the No. 1 song was "The Way We Were" by Barbra Streisand. Ringo Starr had a hit with "You're Sixteen" and some of my friends had been pressing me to go see *Deep Throat II*.

On that day I had been working as John's assistant for about five months. My job every Saturday was to get into the office early and put the finishing touches on Sunday's sports section. That entailed a little writing, a bit of editing, and then heading to the print shop.

I hadn't gotten to the final step when the phone on my desk rang. That wasn't totally unusual because a stringer would occasionally call with a correction, but this was really late morning.

When I picked it up, the woman on the other end asked if she was speaking to Terry Boers. I said yes. She told me she was from St. James Hospital and that my dad had been in an accident. She urged me to get there quickly.

The hospital was only about two blocks from the *Star* office, so I made a few necessary phone calls before I left and headed out, overcome by an immediate sense of dread.

When I got to St. James I was given directions to the intensive care unit. Just as I arrived, I saw a man in scrubs pushing a gurney heading in my direction.

As he got closer, I could see the man on the gurney was my dad. I'll never forget that horrible sight. He was already blue in the face and barely recognizable. When the man realized what was happening, he pulled the sheet over the body.

I remember dropping to my knees in that hallway, already in some form of hysteria. Finally, the gurney guy and a few nurses managed to get me to my feet and into a small office.

Now, I pride myself in keeping my composure and wits even in the most difficult times, but not that day. I wailed that afternoon, feeling as if I'd been gut-punched. I just couldn't get my breath. Even after I had calmed down enough to call my wife with the news, my insides were still churning. I just couldn't get the grip I so desperately needed. When I reached out to my late mom's sister, Ethel, I did it again. I told my aunt what happened and then repeated over and over and over and over how much I needed her help, how much I was hurting, that I couldn't possibly do it by myself.

Not long after that one of the nurses gave me just enough of a sedative to allow me to function, to complete some paperwork, to do what I had to do.

My dad was just 56 years old when he died, the exact same age as my mom, who'd been gone since May of 1972.

And the only accident the day he died came in the yards of Dixie Dairy where he worked. He'd been moving a truck when it suddenly shot forward across the small area and hit another truck. He'd suffered a massive heart attack, most likely before he even hit the other truck. Even in that moment of deep despair, I was hit by an off thought: I hoped the truck he was driving was clean, the way he liked them. I knew at that very moment that I was going be okay, that somewhere down deep I was still me.

Even so, I don't remember all that much about the next three or four days. I do recall greeting many of the guys my dad worked with and other family members, all of whom assured me how much my dad was loved.

Later that evening, I noticed that John E. Meyers and his wife had come in. Now, five months isn't a long time to get to know each other, particularly when the most important lesson is to do things the way John wanted them done. And I mean exactly.

John was kind and consoling, letting me know that I could take as much time as I needed before coming back to work. His wife, Katherine, was equally gracious.

I want to say I was back to work about a week later, that once the initial shock wore off, I was eager to get back, to continue my learning process. More importantly I had to do something besides stewing in my own juices.

And John was ready, too.

He was just as demanding as he'd ever been, but it seemed as if he'd suddenly become more patient with my frequent mistakes. I struggled with a lot of stuff, mostly, as I mentioned, because John wanted all of it done his way.

And believe this, he read every word I wrote on my old IBM Selectric typewriter, painstakingly pointing out what was wrong, what I should have done.

Yes, he was a tough guy with an unparalleled eye for detail. I fully understand how thickheaded I can be at times, but I knew deep down he never made a change that wasn't right.

Truth is, I needed every bit of what he had to offer and I greedily absorbed every last bit of his knowledge, learning to appreciate how valuable all of it was. A pretty wise choice considering John had been doing his job since the 1930s.

And just as importantly, our personal relationship changed within that first year on the job.

Yes, I was still the rather raw recruit to John's drill sergeant, but gradually we drew closer and closer.

That once definitive line between us had blurred. Instead of dissecting every bit of the work, we started to have a good time. The laughter from the far left-hand corner of the office where our desks were situated became a constant. I know it bothered others at times, but no one dared say anything to John.

Even the crustiest of the crusty around the office knew better, although there were more than a few disapproving looks cast in my direction practically every day. I got used to it.

Once, when John was on vacation, the editor of the paper called me into his office to inform me that the time had come to "broaden my horizons," noting that I appeared to have too much time on my hands.

And just how, I wondered, was that going to happen.

He would do so by having me cover a meeting of the Park Forest Zoning Board. I would have sooner been boiled in fucking oil—but I did what was asked. It was two hours of torture you can never get back.

When John returned a few days later, I told him what had happened. And, yes, I was a whiny little tattletale bitch.

John marched into the editor's office and emerged about 30 seconds later. "That will never happen again," he said. And it didn't.

Miraculously, even without my horizons growing broader, I began to flourish. For the first time in my life I had grown completely confident in every newspaper task that would come my way. No more second-guessing. No more angst about a story lede that just didn't sound right.

And John noticed too.

Not all that far into 1975 he told me that he had the okay to do what would be called the Sunday Football Special. All of the teams from the circulation area of the *Star-Tribune* newspapers would be included in that section.

"I want you to design the section, and make it look different than any other part of the paper," John said.

I had quite the haircut when I joined the *Chicago Heights Star* in 1974.

So I did. It was a ton of work to get the look of the section down, plus there was also coordinating the work of all the stringers who covered games for us.

Talk about a labor of love. To this day it was the best project I ever undertook in the newspaper business and the most rewarding. The new-look section was born to rave reviews, especially from John.

But life changes quickly. Within the next year or so, there came the birth of my second son, Joe, and the awful news that my first son, John, was diagnosed with leukemia.

Again, John made my life as easy as possible, telling me to take whatever days off I needed. And I needed a ton of them as it turned out. We tried to balance the needs of an infant with the demands of making sure we got John to Children's Memorial Hospital for his weekly visits.

But you already know that story. In the end, everything would turn out just fine, and no one was happier than John E.

By the time we got to 1978 I knew it was time to look for a job that paid more money. Our financial situation just wasn't good. Too many bills, too little money, and the raises I had received from the *Star* had reached the point where no new money was in sight.

Soon after, Joe Urshel, who'd left the *Star* for the *Detroit Free Press* a few years before, called and said the Freep was looking for someone to work in the features department. He asked me if I was interested. I told him I indeed was. You see, I'd already been told by the *Chicago Sun-Times* that I couldn't be hired unless I had the additional experience of another major metropolitan daily under my belt.

I was eventually hired by the *Free Press*, but it wasn't in features. It was in sports. And the guy who made that decision was

Kurt Luedtke, who just a few years later would co-write the movie *Absence of Malice*. It was the strangest interview I would ever have in my life, but Luedtke got it right. And I thank him.

As I prepared to leave in September, John, who'd turned down every overture from larger papers, including the old *Daily News*, surprised me by writing a column about the time we'd spent together.

To this day it remains the nicest thing anyone has even written about me, noting particularly "how we laughed, oh, how we laughed." He ended it by saying that Terry Boers now "belongs to the world."

I don't think that quite happened, but our last hug was both tearful and joyous. He wanted the best for me, even if the parting hurt so deeply. When John died in 1996 I attended his services and left feeling sadder than I had been in more than 20 years.

There are all kinds of dads these days. Stepdads. Divorced dads. Single dads. Stay-at-home dads. Deadbeat dads, etc.

Saying someone was like a second father sounds a bit trite these days. It's been thrown around so much by so many we've grown somewhat immune. But that's what John E. was.

Let me just note that I loved my father dearly and I still think of him at some point in most days.

John E. Meyers will always be a part of my life, too.

Without his amazing ability to teach, there wouldn't have been a job at the *Free Press*, the *Sun-Times,* or even The Score.

During some of the most tumultuous times of my life he was there for me. And he will forever be in my heart as the greatest newspaper man I have ever known. He was a true gift to the world, and the man most responsible for the success I've had.

chapter 14

The Shows Go On

I would have never guessed back in those early days that Boers and Bernstein would become the standard bearer for the station, that over a period of time we'd become a program consistently rated in the Top 5 amongst men 25-54, that the great change of 1999 would claim us as the only true success story.

North's solo show in the mornings didn't really fly with the listeners, nor did it help much when he added a co-host here and there. Whatever the combination, it just didn't work. And North didn't seem to do himself any favors, branching off into topics that would land him in hot water more than once.

The 4 PM to 8 PM McNeil-Jiggetts show was doomed from the beginning. Danny didn't have much interest in making it a success and that message was clear when you listened. His idea of what made good radio just didn't go along with that of Jiggetts, who would push on by himself for a time after Danny left to do afternoons at ESPN 1000, where we would eventually become rivals. But let's not get too far ahead of ourselves here.

Danny's move in 2000 shocked no one who knew him. He was absolutely miserable and quickly took the first safety net provided him. Given the circumstances, I think any of us would have done the same. He lobbied for different hours, but his pleas were continually rejected. I knew the move was coming, it was just a matter of to where and when.

I recall there were outside rumors of the turmoil going on at the station, but I've always felt that falling into that trap was counterproductive. I don't mind a little office politics here and there when the time is right, but this, at least in my mind, was not the time. Bernstein and I hadn't established a damn thing to that point, so we needed to worry about ourselves, even as the belief grew that the station was collapsing around us.

I thought we were getting better, but I didn't have any tangible proof until the world stopped turning (thank you, Alan Jackson) on September 11, 2001, when the World Trade Center was attacked.

That was about the only day of my life where I just couldn't do my radio job. I left shortly after the second tower collapsed, driving home so dazed I couldn't tell you to this very day what roads I took home.

Only in the aftermath of that tragedy did it finally hit me that we were fully capable of doing a great radio show, no matter what the circumstances. While both of us felt angry and hurt just like most Americans, we somehow found the right words to use, touching the same nerves that were being tested around the country. We had good interaction with callers, something that wasn't necessarily normal, but it actually happened.

I didn't think about any of this until much later. We just wanted to get through the aftermath clean, waiting for that moment when it would be okay to laugh again. David Letterman provided that answer on September 17 at the end of a brilliantly delivered monologue when he sideswiped his buddy Regis Philbin.

Perhaps I'm being a bit too simplistic here, but if we could handle some of the darkest days in American history, we could certainly handle a Bears Monday after a loss.

That's not to say that the inmates weren't still running the asylum in many instances, but I knew that if we weren't already the best show on the station, it would only be a matter of time before people recognized that fact.

As it was, the 21st century was proving problematical for us in a lot of ways. North continued to flounder in the mornings, even as we made our way from the Belmont Bunker to the spacious NBC Tower. Murph was still on his way to becoming a douchebag for the ages, doing it along with Fred Huebner, who provided him with some actual names of people involved in sports who weren't Cubs.

We were in our spot and the afternoons now belonged to *Sun-Times* columnist Rick Telander, who'd occasionally bring his guitar to the studio, just in case a hootenanny were to break out. Along with him was everybody's favorite Doug Buffone and Jonathan Hood, a former Boers and Bernstein producer.

Perhaps the saddest sight I ever saw came at the 2005 Super Bowl in Jacksonville, Florida, when we were making our way down radio row to see where we were broadcasting from.

Aside from being booked into a Jacksonville crack house passing as a hotel, the sight of Hood sitting at the end of the table, idly reading a newspaper while Telander conducted an interview was galling, to say the least. I knew that was the case, but seeing it was worse. Paul Agase didn't want Hood to participate in any interviews. What a load of shit. J. Hood was—and is—a bright and funny guy who knows what he's doing. Telander certainly could have stood up for Hood and told Agase he welcomed everyone's participation. But he chose not to. Dope.

I'll never understand why any of this was allowed to happen, although I know why it happened. Agase, The Score's general manager at the time, was the son of Alex Agase, who was Telander's football coach at Northwestern. I'm sure poorer decisions have been made, but this was a doozy.

Sporting that 1970s 'stache.

It's also something that I've never let Paul forget to this very day. Telander may have been a lot of things to a lot of people, but in order to be a radio personality, you actually have to have one.

Telander would later become a constant target on our show not for being an awful host (well, maybe a dig every so often) but rather his idiotic stance from roughly 2012 to 2015 when he claimed he didn't understand what the Cubs' gameplan was for the future.

And Telander's exit was every bit as bizarre as his fucked-up show. He announced his resignation on the air without telling anyone at the station of his intent. He said it was just too much to do a talk show and a column. And can you imagine how much more difficult it would be if he were actually good at either job?

Anyway, this mess fell into the lap of Mitch Rosen, who'd recently become The Score's program director, a job he'd held at ESPN 1000.

Being the smart guy that he is, Mitch wasn't the least bit put out by Telander's decision. He didn't get into the cartwheel line or anything like most of us did, but his reaction was completely professional, although he would later tell me Telander's departure was one of the best things that ever happened to The Score.

Mike Mulligan, along with Buffone, took over the afternoon show and did just fine. Mully would eventually move to mornings in September of 2009 where he'd be teamed with Brian Hanley. They're still going strong.

At the same time, Mitch moved Dan and I back to afternoons, the time slot I loved the most, the spot where I'd longed for another chance to compete with every other show on the same level. No more saying goodbye at 4:30, no more wondering if people could hear us in the western suburbs. I was ready. Dan was ready.

There's plenty of reasons why Mitch has succeeded to such a high level in a very tough business, but the guy has a heart of pure gold. He will fight for you in every way possible, always worrying that his on-air people are happy.

I've mentioned that I've had some sensational bosses over the years, guys who went to bat for me, who stuck with me when it might have been easier to choose another path.

I never worried about that with Mitch. He had my back from the first day he took the job to the last day I worked on Jan. 5, 2017. And he still does to this very minute. You just can't ask for much more. All I can say is I love him, and you'd love him too if you got to know him.

Longtime producers Matt Abbatacola (far left) and Chris Tannehill (far right) pose with me and Dan Bernstein during my final broadcast. *(Courtesy of 670 The Score)*

All right, back to B&B. Our listenership remained solid and we kept adding more and more to the show along the way, including the ever-widening Friday Fung segment, which had been inspired by then White Sox manager Ozzie Guillen. The guests executive producer Matt Abbatacola helped put together for the all-important football season also improved drastically over the years. Our college and pro experts were as good as anyone out there, and all possessed a keen insight while understanding that it's okay to be entertaining, too.

But even as all of that was falling together over the years, Bernstein remained a hot topic not only with the listeners, but even at CBS where longtime employees would occasionally tell me how sorry they were that I had to put up with him on a daily basis.

On remotes, he quickly climbed to No. 2 on my most asked question list. Right behind "Is Murph that big of an asshole?" was "Is Dan that much of a jackoff?"

My answers, in order, were yes and no.

The primary complaint against Bernstein over the years is that he wasn't nice to the callers. Being a guy that had plenty of run-ins with listeners in my 25 years, I'd be a complete hypocrite to knock him for that. I don't suffer fools gladly. Never have, never will. What Dan enabled me to do in most cases was just kick back and enjoy him going after somebody. Let me rephrase that. I loved it. Let him do the heavy lifting. I would occasionally chime in, but in many cases I didn't feel the need, especially since many of them were gone in an instant.

Nowhere was it written in my contract that you have to coddle dumb guys or those who are simply looking for a fight by being outrageous. There are no hard and fast rules involving such things. Everything is done at your own discretion. Sure, there are things that are positively verboten. Thankfully, torturing the stupid isn't on the list.

And if you caught ESPN's 30 for 30 "Mike and the Mad Dog," you probably heard the guy say he didn't like them because they weren't "nice to their listeners." That's interesting, considering the two are probably the most popular sports radio show ever put together, dominating the ratings like few have when WFAN opened for business in 1987.

It should also be noted that there were other listeners who were absolutely delighted that callers got an occasional kick in the ass.

My money says that's the prevailing sentiment.

The one quibble I had with the whole thing was the insistence that the WFAN show spawned a bunch of people on the airwaves around the country who were trying to copy Chris Russo. It was during that particularly segment that they showed a clip of North and Jiggetts from the early days at The Score. Not only is that unfair, it's just not true. North wasn't copying anyone. He was just being himself. Believe me, the North on the air was no different than the North off the air.

It all gets back to that fragile chemistry thing. Some lab experiments work, many more don't. I know both of us wanted to succeed and would do whatever it took. I'm proud to say we were the lone success story following the changes made in 1999. I can honestly say that I never even snapped at Dan until our last Super Bowl trip in January 2016 to San Francisco. Even then it wasn't on the air, although we certainly had our share of disagreements over the years. This was just about Dan acting as if Chris Tannehill and I had never been anywhere, that we needed him to set a minute-by-minute social calendar. We didn't.

And while Abbatacola famously didn't much care for Bernstein, that didn't really matter in the big picture. Anybody who listened on a regular basis knew that was the case, and, no, Matt wasn't lying and he didn't hold back at any point as he became the longest-tenured EP we'd ever had.

I've always thought that if the show is good enough, that kind of stuff only adds a little spice. Were there times when it became a little uncomfortable for me? Sure. But I also knew that if the two were bickering, the quality of the show wouldn't suffer. A lot of folks over the years told me they loved it, no matter how cringe-worthy it got.

The only change we had in the last number of years came when our guy Jason Goff, once renowned as young Jason from Evanston when he would call the old afternoon show back in the '90s, left his producer's job to take a show in Atlanta.

It was the right thing to do. Jason was ready then and he's been terrific since he came back to the station to work middays with Matt Spiegel and, ultimately, take my place alongside Bernstein in afternoons.

How lucky were we? Lucky enough to get Chris Tannehill, the best radio soundman in the business, who was waiting in the wings to replace him. With Tannehill came a wall of remarkable sound, but also one of the nicest guys you'll ever meet.

Actually, I was blessed during my 45-year career in newspapers and radio to be surrounded by people I genuinely liked, at least for the most part. There were a few ass monkeys along the way, but you expect that.

When I started my first newspaper job at the *Lansing Sun-Journal* in June 1972, one of the first guys I met was named Randy Hellman, the editor of the Lansing paper and, are you ready for this, *The Harvey News Bee*. Tall and slender, Randy was, in the vernacular of the times, the coolest cat in the room. And I mean any room.

I might have been the ugliest cat, the dumbest cat, the guy most likely to smell like kitty litter, but Randy was the goods. The women all loved him and he commanded tremendous respect in general from even the oldest veterans at the paper, although he was just a few years older than me.

Turns out he'd been a helluva pitcher when he was kid, and he came from an athletic family, especially his dad, Kenneth. The elder Hellman had been a starter on the 1933 state basketball champion Thornton Wildcats high school team, who'd become known as The Flying Clouds. The star of that team was another pretty good athlete too, a fellow by the name of Lou Boudreau, who would go on to play a little baseball in his life.

I have a picture taken in early July of '72, meaning I'd been at the *Sun-Journal* for less than a month. There I am on the far left, hair in my eyes and wearing the dress code, a shirt and tie. Randy is standing next to me looking more than a little nonchalant for the staff meeting, although he was conforming to the code.

Aside from managing editor James Alvord, Randy and I are the only men in the picture. Maybe that's why we bonded. Not sure, but it makes sense. I was still trying to get over the death of my mother in May and not doing all that well at times. Randy, of course, was free and easy.

He was all about having fun. I can't begin to tell you how many hours after work we spent at a bar in Lansing, but we weren't getting hammered. We were playing the electronic Darto game (I think that's what it was called). I'd beat him every so often, but he was way better at it than me.

Do that long enough and sooner or later you're going to share your deepest, darkest secrets. Naturally, his were better than mine, but no one was keeping score. We were just growing into a friendship that I believed was going to last a lifetime.

I would soon enough meet his stunning fiancée, whom he planned to marry within a year or so.

But none of it ever happened. By July of '73, Randy Hellman, despite fighting like hell, was dead from an aggressive form of cancer that really never gave him a chance. I was crushed. I'd never fully processed my mom's death and now this.

I remember attending Randy's services in South Holland. I don't think I'd ever been to anything quite like it. So sad. So dreadful for everyone who loved him. I remember leaving the funeral home and promising myself that I would never, ever let anyone I worked with get that close again. It might not have been the smartest choice or certainly the most adult, but I couldn't do it again, at least not with anyone who was close to my age.

I eventually did start to allow people back in, most notably Abbatacola, but it never came easy. Generally there's a price for everything.

chapter 15

To the Motor City and Back

The ground rules set for me when I arrived at the *Detroit Free Press* in September 1978 to work the sports desk were simple. Do what you're told and don't ever ask to write. And not necessarily in that order.

I readily gave my word on that to a terrific newspaperman named Ken Clover, who would later take me on a trip to the two hottest spots I needed to know in downtown Motown—the Anchor Bar and the Lindell A.C., which was owned by the legendary Jimmy Butsicaris. I met Jimmy the first night Clover took me in, and Jimmy was quick to point out exactly where in the bar then Twins manager Billy Martin had beaten the living crap out of Minnesota pitcher Dave Boswell in 1969.

"Boswell deserved it," Butsicaris said. "He'd sucker-punched [outfielder Bob] Allison and Billy let him have it after Boswell took a swing at him."

Butsicaris then pantomimed the series of punches that Martin had landed, complete with sound effects. After that first night,

Butsicaris was never a stranger. He remembered everything and everybody, although most of guys on the desk I ran with preferred the Anchor, a dive's dive just a few blocks away. You see, there was this great old pinball machine in the place that easily gobbled up the three hours we had to kill between the State and Metro editions.

What we gobbled up is open to your conjecture. And let the record show that I never did ask Clover for a writing assignment. I enjoyed working on that desk, even as the low man. Not only did we have fun, I was proving, at least to my satisfaction, that I belonged, that I could handle the pressure and the workload without needing someone to hold my hand every second.

Did I handle all the deadline stuff flawlessly? Probably not. I don't know that anyone does. But I knew that things were going to be just fine when longtime slot guy Ken Kramer stopped yelling at me. He was actually a helluva guy. He just didn't like stupid mistakes, especially the same ones over and over.

Meanwhile, I was driving home every weekend and my memory of the winter of '78 is nothing but nasty. More than once during that trip down good old I-94 I was caught in a snowstorm, an ice storm, and/or just about any other kind of wintry hell you can think of, but this wasn't one of those choice things. I wanted to see Carolyn and my two sons. It made those weekends special. Short, but special.

With all that going on, I didn't have five minutes to think about writing, at least not my own. When I give one of those solemn promises as I had to Clover, it was over in my mind, territory that I wouldn't revisit. And it didn't bother me in the least. There was no itch that needed scratching, no desire that made the desk work seems tedious, although there is no doubt plenty of tedium built in.

Besides, by the spring of 1979 we had sold our house in Matteson and cobbled together enough money so that we could rent this sprawling, old-style ranch house in Redford. John's care was shifted to the University of Michigan hospital in Ann Arbor and Joe was busy building his résumé as one of the craziest two-year-olds on the planet.

Ofttimes, Joe would leave both of us speechless after one of his many forays into the personal whacky space where he seemed to thrive. His favorite move was throwing crackers at unsuspecting people in restaurants. You might remember that there once was a time when most eateries would put out a bowlful of crackers. Hell, even Pizza Hut did it, if I remember correctly. There was just a couple in each package, so they weren't going to injure anyone. But it was annoying to us and others. I think we finally broke him of that habit when he was 24. Just kidding.

By that time 1 had settled nicely into the *Free Press*, playing a little softball with the company team at times, although nothing ever came close to matching the hectic softball schedule I had once kept in Chicago.

We all got used to living in Detroit, although the lack of quality pizza was a problem, as was the inability to find a great beef sandwich. There, is that Chicago enough for you?

But more importantly, work was going great. I learned to love the Kens, Clover and Kramer, as well as guys like Wylie Gerdes, Brian Bragg, and Norbert Siwa, who'd been on the desk forever. They were all solid guys who knew their stuff, and we'd long ago became friends.

I couldn't tell you if I was great at the job, good at job, or just managing to keep my head above water. I wasn't getting any complaints, and when you work on the desk that's about as good as it gets.

Finally, and rather unexpectedly, Clover came to me in mid-August of '79 and asked if I wanted a writing assignment. That topic hadn't been broached in almost a year, so I wasn't sure if this was just a test of my loyalty to the job I had, or if he'd actually been thinking about this.

To be honest, I didn't think I'd shown that much on the desk. There was always rewriting this or that, but it wasn't splashy. Just doing the job.

What Clover wanted me to do seemed simple enough. Cover a small-college football game in a few weeks and submit 300 words before the 6 PM deadline for the state edition.

I told him I would do it. And as it turned out, it could have been the last writing assignment I ever had.

Carolyn and I on our honeymoon in 1974 at the Fairmount Hotel in San Francisco.

I don't know if it was writer's block or pure nerves, but I barely managed to make deadline, sitting in front of a blank computer screen for the better part of three hours. Cobbling together 300 words on a game that was won on a last-second field goal isn't difficult. It's something I'd been doing for the better part of eight years with little or no trouble.

I made the deadline with about a minute to spare, figuring that was going to be about it. I would be the one—and done—story guy. Just a footnote.

When I saw Clover on Monday, he said, "Thanks for making deadline."

I figured that was it. I was cooked. Fuck me very much.

About two days later Clover told me I'd be doing Michigan State home football games in the fall and some weekend Tigers home games, giving Jim Hawkins a break. I couldn't believe all was forgiven. So I thanked Clover. Over and over.

IT WAS JUST a month or so later that the *Sun-Times* reentered the picture, keeping the promise they'd made. And that offer came less than one week after we finally sold our home in Matteson and bought a nice place in Livonia, Michigan, only a few miles from the rental home in Redford. Bad timing, indeed.

Carol and I would be separated again, just as we had been when the *Free Press* job began. I'd lived with Joe Urshel and his wife, Donna, in Birmingham, then moved into an East Detroit apartment with another friend of mine from the *Free Press*. And yes, the whole America's guest thing was getting old. But if you can't afford to pay two rents, you were at the mercy of others' charity.

So here we go again. I moved in with my late aunt's second husband, who just happened to live in the same place Carol and I had lived briefly after we were married in February 1971. Talk about old home week.

Uncle Johnny was a great guy and a better roomie. Why? Because he was never home during the day and my hours were 3 PM to 11:30. Also, because dear Johnny had what we called the crooked elbow. The guy could drink. And drink. Get the picture?

And while the *Sun-Times* desk was filled by a ton of veteran newspapermen, including George Vass and Don Edwards, there was plenty of room for a 29-year-old idiot who was still willing to stop, look, and listen when the proper time arrived.

Oh, and there was one other thing. Sports editor Marty Kaiser, yet another really good guy, made me promise that I would never ask him to write. I readily agreed. I wish I could say that I knew my chance would come, but I didn't. Nor did I particularly care. I wasn't sure that writing was the be-all, end-all thing in the first place, so at no point did I grow restless or bored. Wanderlust just wasn't my thing. At least I didn't think so then.

BUT SOON ENOUGH I would find myself in the middle of what I consider to be greatest decade of sports in history. I'm not trying to start one those ridiculous contrarian arguments that have soiled the sports landscape in recent years. I'm just making a case for a decade that began with the biggest upset in the history, aka The Miracle on Ice, and ended with baseball's all-time hit king being banned for life for betting on baseball. Can you top that? Maybe in your world, but not in mine.

And what happened in between wasn't too shabby, either. And for some of it I had a front-row seat….Please allow me to explain.

It was just a few days before Paul Westhead, a space cadet to beat all space cadets, was about to officially become the head coach of the Chicago Bulls in June of 1982. The *Sun-Times* was set to hire Richard Justice of the *Houston Chronicle* to take over the Chicago Bulls beat. It was just a day before Justice was due to come into town to accept the gig when he called Kaiser to say he had changed his mind, that he would instead be taking a job with the *Washington Post* to cover baseball, which was his first love.

It was a good deal for Richard, who's spent more than 30 years covering major league baseball since then. It was, however, a bad deal for Kaiser and the *Sun-Times* because not only was the paper left in the proverbial lurch, but Marty was offended, just as anyone would have been.

He was also stuck. No one who had any sort of national reputation was going to take the job on such short notice. So how stuck was he?

Stuck enough to call me into his office and offer me the job. Now that is stuck. Other than rewriting Dave Feldman columns and the assorted works of my buddy, the late Rev. Lacy J. Banks., the only thing I'd done creatively was put together the sports people column for the next day's paper.

But that job was almost 100 percent silly. I didn't look for any items with depth, I sought out the stupid and wrote it that way. For that reason alone I looked forward to doing it.

This, however, was a whole new animal. It was the daily grind of covering a team, of being at every practice, every game, and criss-crossing the country in the process. Did I believe I could do it? Yes, I did. But that was based on absolutely nothing concrete in the way of proof.

Although he had every right to be uptight about the whole mess, Marty didn't seem a bit nervous when he made me the offer. Now, I've always believed that he had to have done so with great trepidation. I remember having plenty. But the bottom line was this: the job was worth an upgrade in pay, something that would soon come in handy.

I accepted the job. I didn't even tease Marty by asking him if it was now okay for me to write.

A day later, on June 23, 1982, I was at Paul Westhead's introductory press conference, noting he was a Shakesperean scholar who didn't seem to understand what to be and what not to be.

Westhead, who'd won a title with the Lakers in 1980 before Magic Johnson decided he wanted him canned, wanted the Bulls to run, run, and then run some more. That was fantasyland crap. He had guys like Dave Corzine, an aging Dwight Jones, and Mark Olberding, another plodder on the roster.

This struck no one as the kind of team that was going to outrun any opponent, although Westhead planned on playing right through those roster flaws with Reggie Theus, Orlando Woolridge, and rookie guard Quintin Dailey, the team's controversial first-round pick.

Westhead was wrong, of course.

The Guru of Go was also the man of going, going gone after just one disastrous 28-win season. But things were about to start getting a lot better in the draft, the one that would put the GOAT in a Bulls uniform.

We'll get to that and a shitload of other stuff in the '80s, but first things first.

chapter 16

Celebrity?

Before I get to this whole silly celebrity, fame thing, can I mention something that absolutely, positively has bugged the living shit out of me for as long as I can remember?

And this used to happen with a startling degree of regularity, no matter if I was at a remote broadcast, a mall, an airport, an OTB, a movie, or even out to dinner. It seemed there was always someone who would invariably saunter up and say, "Do you remember me?"

Now, it would be fine if they'd said I'm so and so and you might remember me from such and such a place, but to just say, "Do you remember me?"

For fuck's sake what's wrong with you?

And I'm not just talking about doing it to me, I'm talking about doing it to anybody. Is it so hard to have the common courtesy to re-introduce yourself without the bullshit and games?

The even bigger picture here is that more than once someone has done it to me and I absolutely had no idea who they were, and, on more than one occasion, they seemed genuinely hurt by the perceived slight, even if completely unintended.

Too goddamn bad.

Maybe next time they'll handle themselves the right way. Maybe they'll handle the situation like a true adult.

And as if you couldn't tell, let the record show I don't have a great memory for faces and I never have, so I know it's not a function of getting older or crabbier or crazier because I still have a vivid recollection of some events from decades ago. But even if I had the best memory in the history of memories, I don't know if I could possibly file away every person I've met the last five years, let alone the last 10 or 20 or 30 or 40. My best guesstimate is that I've probably pressed the flesh of 25,000 or so people in the last 25 years.

I won't apologize for that. Now, if I were the Amazing Kreskin, who was a late-night TV regular in the '70s and just a tad creepy, I'd say my bad. Kreskin, FYI, billed himself as a mentalist. He'd been inspired by the famous comic strip Mandrake the Magician written by Lee Falk. Now this Mandrake dude was a serious crime fighter. The only thing I've ever made disappear over the years are listeners.

Anyway, Carol and I were in an establishment in Orland Park a number of years ago, sitting at a table adjacent to the bar. That's when a guy walked up to us and posed the question I hate.

I said I honestly didn't remember him, to give me some help.

He said who he was and I certainly remembered the name because I'd worked with him at the *Sun-Times*, and we had indeed been friendly. But I hadn't seen him in more than 25 years and he'd put on a bunch of weight.

Anyway, he immediately launched into an idiotic hissy fit, actually saying to Carol, "I used to know your husband when he was a nice guy."

I'd tell you who this guy was but you wouldn't know the name anyway. So to him and all others with zero manners, here's a simple message: GO FUCK YOURSELF.

Sorry, having a bad memory isn't a character flaw and it certainly doesn't give anyone the right to act like a raging asshole. And I'll never change my mind about that.

TO BE PERFECTLY honest, there are times when it comes to dealing with people that I also fell well short of the rules I just put down. I'd guess that roughly 15 percent of time when someone comes up to me and asks, "Are you Terry Boers?" I'll say no. I'd mentioned on the air more than once in my last four years or so, that I would only answer if you called me Edward Dickman.

Okay, maybe that's a character flaw, but I choose to call it a quirk. It certainly avoids a conversation I don't want. Maybe all that's required is a simple hello, but I don't know that, so I just thought I'd have some fun.

What inspired all this? Well, it should be noted that more than once I've had a guy sit down at a dinner table I'm sharing with family members. And stay seated as if he'd been invited.

Now aside from the chutzpah it takes to do such a thing—the words chuckleheaded cocksucker come to mind—what would possess anyone to do such a thing?

So please let the record show that when I'm done working for the day I don't want to talk sports, unless we're at an event. I don't even want a 10-second discussion on the Bears or the Cubs or the White Sox or Hawks or anyone else once work is done.

Moreover, I don't think it's possible to be careful enough these days. I've angered more than my share of people over the years,

Celebrating the 15th anniversary of the Boers and Bernstein Show in 2014. *(Courtesy of 670 The Score)*

whether it was roasting them on the air or simply having a different opinion on any of the hot-button issues we've covered.

Am I afraid at times? I wouldn't say afraid, but I don't think it hurts to be cautious, particularly when people you don't know a thing about can walk right up to you at a remote.

Please note that never in the history of The Score have we ever had anything even remotely resembling security when we were on site. If someone has a grudge, any of us at the station can be found without much effort. About the only time in the 2000s the threats got a bit scary came after racing legend Dale Earnhardt crashed and died at the 2001 Daytona 500. Bernstein and I made fun of people who were having a hard time dealing with the fact that he was dead, despite having hit the wall at 200 mph while attempting to block for racing partner Michael Waltrip, who would win the storied race.

Bernstein had a security guard walk him to his car in the face of some threats. Thankfully, nothing ever happened, the best-case scenario for everyone involved.

As for the members of NASCAR Nation, we learned firsthand what crazy looks like and sounds like. I'm not saying that there aren't other fandoms just as frightening, but the NASCAR whack jobs had no problem taking this from 0 to 150 seemingly in a matter of days. Wait, check that, in a matter of moments.

What's strange here is that we had Dale Earnhardt Jr. on the show a number of years later and he was an absolute delight to visit with. He gets it 100 percent, seemingly having as much fun with us as we did with him. You can also put Junior on the very smart list. He announced his retirement from the sport in 2017 after battling the effects of two debilitating concussions he'd suffered in 2016.

We visited with a number of NASCAR's best over the years, thanks to our association with the folks at the Joliet Motor Speedway.

They were all fun and interesting, especially to someone who enjoys catching a race here and there.

Again, I credit The Score for taking such fast action back in 2001 in the wake of the many threats that came pouring in. But please understand this, I'm not sure that any station provides crowd control no matter where they're broadcasting from.

Still, there's a positive here. In the early days of the station one of our annual summer remote stops was the Taste of Chicago. That was even the case when I was a regular on The Sportswriters Sunday afternoons on WGN from 1988 to 1991.

Now if you're looking to see the sorriest, hillbilliest, smelliest group of people on the planet, the Taste is clearly the place. I mean, seriously, we're supposedly promoting the station to the criminally obese in tube tops and butt-crack shorts.

And don't let me get started on the men.

Suffice to say, my days of actually attending sporting events in Chicago—unless something very weird happens—are finished.

I don't remember the last time I did it just for fun. My guess it was years ago when my kids were little. I will, however, do it in Florida, where my anonymity remains mostly intact.

But enough of that.

Let's get to the real gist of this celebrity thing.

DESPITE BEING THE third-largest market in the country and still the best big city of them all (if you can ignore the body count), I'll grant you that we seem to fall short in the celebrity category.

Sure, we are the home of former President Barack Obama, but he's not really from Chicago. He just moved here.

Same goes for Oprah Winfrey, easily one of the most egotistical women in the history of the world. A real Pecksniff. But that's just me. When Oprah announced in 2009 that she was going to close down her dog and pony show in 2011, she left behind millions of sobbing, silly ass, middle-aged women to wonder what they were going to do with their lives.

My first reaction when I heard Oprah say she was retiring was to scream "YESSSSSS" at the top of my lungs.

Then Mayor Richard M. Daley, aka Captain Numb Nuts, laid the blame for The Really Big O's decision on the evil media, noting that a person can only take so much before they get fed up.

Right. I'm sure it's been a tremendous burden on Oprah to have her ass kissed 24/7. I think her replacement should have been the wheelbarrow of fat she rolled out years ago to demonstrate how much weight she'd lost.

So what does that leave us with?

Well, you always have the athletes, and there are plenty of them here, although none of them are all that exciting when you consider this was once the home of worldwide superstar Michael Jordan.

I'm sure onetime Bears quarterback Jay Cutler enjoyed some of his time in Chicago, but I never sensed he was completely comfortable here before he and his vacuous wife headed off to Nashville and quickly landed an NFL broadcasting gig for Fox before putting those plans on hold to sign on with the Miami Dolphins.

We do have a couple of completely annoying acting fucks around in Jim Belushi and John Cusack, but by far the coolest local guy of them all, William Peterson, doesn't really want the attention, either.

The onetime star of the CBS mega hit *CSI*, Billy Pete tells the story of walking around downtown seeing the sights with some friends and family from out of town when he suddenly realized that he had a crowd of people following him around. He said it was "uncomfortable."

And this, again, comes from one of the nicest guys you're ever going to meet.

Politicians? Does anybody really want to be identified with the low-life scumbags Chicago and the state of Illinois produce?

Of course, there are always exceptions, but I think the smart people in the state want many of these beady-eyed bastards to just go away.

So just to cut the list short, let's say we're down to TV and radio.

By TV, I mean mostly the news folks. Anything that's locally produced other than the news is generally horseshit.

It isn't that most of them I've met over the years aren't nice enough people, in the main they have been. But are they big-time celebs?

Well, maybe they have to be.

So now we're down to radio, more specifically sports radio.

And I mean down.

Perhaps because I've sat on one too many radio rows at Super Bowls, I've come to the sad understanding that the sports radio world is inundated with sad, goofy-looking bastards who scream too much and generally appear to have bad hygiene.

Now you could go ahead and say you're better than that, but you do the same damn thing for a living. I don't know if that pig-faced guy from Jacksonville we ran into at the Super Bowl is a big deal. I don't even know if he's still alive. Is Nasty Nestor hot shit? Is he alive? We know Mike Francesa from The Fan in New York is the star of stars to many talk-radio types, but how big a deal is he in a city loaded with stars? And how big would he be if he actually stayed awake while he was on the air? Yes, he's been known to doze off upon occasion.

Trust me, there's never been a minute spent in my life where I've sat around thinking I'm some kind of big deal.

I'm not. And never have been. Just ask Edward Dickman.

chapter 17

Covering the 1980s

So where did we leave off...?

Oh, yeah, the 1980s. But before I get back to that, remember I'd suffered a horrific brain fart that had almost caused me to miss a deadline I should have made with ease.

Thankfully, Clover was going to give me another chance...and this was the one I wanted to make the most of—covering Major League Baseball. I'd loved baseball since I was a little kid, and it was a dream come true when I walked into the old Tiger Stadium on a clear, crisp autumn night to cover a game.

And quite naturally, not a single person at the stadium knew who I was. I arrived early and I distinctly remember the guards at the gate studying my press pass like it was a priceless piece of art.

"So how long you been at the *Free Press*?" one of the ancient satraps asked. "About a year," I replied. "How come I've never heard of you?" he responded.

"Because I haven't been writing that much," I said. "This is my first baseball assignment." He looked at his compatriot. "Should we let him go?" he asked. If you're getting the idea that I was somehow missing the joke here, you'd be correct. Those old fucks got the best of me.

Hell, I can't even remember if the Tigers won (I believe they did), but I certainly remember the postgame. I spent some time in the home locker room before the game, basically just introducing myself to some of the players, including starting pitcher Dan Petry and promising shortstop Alan Trammell, who was in his third year with the Tigers.

I'd said hello to manager Sparky Anderson before the game, but I wanted to check back in with him, just so he'd remember me.

In his first season with the Tigers, Anderson had come to town promising that "If I can't make this club a winner in five years, then I'll walk away and say I failed." As it turned out, Sparky's projection was right on the money. The Tigers would win the World Series in 1984, beating a San Diego Padres team that had bounced back to beat the Cubs after losing the first two games of the NLCS at Wrigley Field.

So what was Sparky doing when I went into his office? Sitting buck naked with his feet up on the desk smoking a pipe. "What do you need?" Sparky said, fully understanding that he had me right where he wanted me. "Nothing, really," I answered. "Just wanted to say I'll see you tomorrow."

The minute I said that I wanted to take it back. I think I'd seen more than enough of him to last for months, perhaps years. "Okay," Anderson said. "Tomorrow it is."

Little did I know that he wasn't the first baseball manager I'd meet who liked being naked. Many names would be added to the list, including guys like John McNamara, Jim Fregosi, and

Don Zimmer. Old time baseball apparently meant pants were optional. Apparently all a part of the undress code.

Okay, now back to the Bulls and Westhead, their new head coach who was about to make the first of his many mistakes when he said training camp would be held in Peoria, getting away from what he called "the glare" of the spotlight.

Uh, no. The only glare was shining on the controversial first-round pick Dailey, who'd come across with a distinct air of indifference about his past when he met the Chicago media for the first time the day after the draft.

His agent, Bob Woolf, would later admit he'd made a huge mistake. Woolf, figuring that Dailey had done just fine with the New York types the night of the draft, had other business to attend to the next day, so he left Dailey on his own.

I would soon make a trip to San Francisco to research Dailey's checkered past, which included the assault of a University of San Francisco nursing student. Dailey had been charged with "assault to commit rape, assault with intent to commit oral copulation, aggravated assault and willful and unlawful violation of personal liberty."

As near as I could tell from my days in Frisco, the overwhelming feeling was that Dailey was 100 percent guilty, at least in the eyes of the people I'd talked to, including law enforcement.

That may have been so, but Dailey wound up pleading guilty to just aggravated assault. The other charges were ultimately dropped. He was given what amounted to a slap on the wrist—three years' probation—and would later settle a civil suit with the woman for $100,000.

That first day in Chicago, Dailey stunned just about everyone. He not only seemed to dismiss the whole matter, he had zero compassion for the victim, saying, "It's a forgotten episode, so I don't concern myself."

You could almost hear the alarm bells going off across the state. The Illinois chapter of the National Organization of Women finally got a meeting with Bulls management in October, recommending that Dailey seek counseling. They also wanted the Bulls management to say they didn't condone violence against women. One of the Bulls' owners, Jonathan Kovler, said at the time he would take it under consideration.

To my knowledge, that never happened. And NOW mobilized, making sure there were protestors in Peoria and there were even more for the home opener at the old Chicago Stadium.

And road games were not a relief, either. Protestors seemed to spring up at every stop and the fans were merciless. That included San Antonio, where two fans, one dressed as a nurse, simulated an assault during the player introductions.

And while Dailey had the ability to put on his air of cool for the most part, there was no doubt in my mind that all of this weighed heavily on him, even if he seemed fine on the court, averaging more than 15 points a game and four assists.

Finally, on Dec. 7, 1982, Dailey failed to show up for a home game vs. the New York Knicks. The first official word was that Dailey had overslept. I would later dig up the fact that general manager Rod Thorn had actually found Dailey hiding in a closet, as if he were seeking refuge from the outside world.

A few days later it was announced that Dailey had been put under the care of a Chicago psychiatrist, and would need ongoing treatment. Dailey was not only suffering from depression, he'd also told Thorn that he wanted to kill himself.

Woolf, who'd become a pretty good friend of mine over the years, said that Dailey had called him sobbing and crying, saying that he wanted to commit suicide. "No doubt in my mind how serious he was," Woolf would later tell me. "I was scared."

About two weeks later it was announced that Dailey would return to the Bulls for a scheduled road game against the Detroit Pistons. Fred Mitchell of the *Tribune* and I were on high alert that night, especially after it was discovered that Dailey would be coming to the hotel bar. I've waited in worse places.

While he was officially being treated for depression, I think anyone who knew the circumstances believed that Dailey also needed help for substance abuse, something that would eventually be addressed.

That night, Dailey strode into the bar and promptly bought a round for all of us, including himself. I remember pulling him aside and asking him off the record if having a drink was the smart thing do. "Why not?" Dailey answered. "Don't believe everything you write."

In the following years, Dailey would go in for rehab on two other occasions. He would also play for the Los Angeles Clippers, the Seattle SuperSonics and, finally, the Yakima Sun Kings before giving up the ghost.

Dailey finally seemed to get his life together in 1996 when he was hired by the Clark County Parks and Recreation Department. He would eventually become a recreation and cultural program supervisor, a position he held until his death in 2010 at the age of 49.

I have wrestled with the Dailey conundrum over the years, just as many have done when it comes to athletes and the many laws some of them don't appear to respect.

In fairness, I can honestly say that I didn't dislike Dailey as a person, judging him solely on our interactions. Did I feel compassion for him? Sympathy? At times. But it was always tempered by that long ago night in San Francisco, when his compassion and human decency deserted him.

Here's the universal truth, at least in my world. It's a helluva lot easier to hate someone if you really don't know them. Or, you could learn to hate them even more if you do have to deal with them. Got it, Bobby Knight?

A final note on the '82-'83 Bulls. Westhead was wrong on just about any level you could imagine. Moving to Peoria didn't do a thing to simmer down the tensions caused by Dailey, and he was just as wrong about his team.

The Guru of Go(ne) was axed after the disastrous 28-win season, which left everyone in the organization with a bad taste in their mouths on several levels. The reward for all that bad was the fifth pick of the draft, which the Bulls used on UNLV forward Sidney Green. But things were about to start getting a lot better in the 1984 draft, the one that would put the GOAT in a Bulls uniform.

We'll get to that, but first let's get to the 1982-83 NBA Finals, which featured the Showtime Lakers vs. Moses Malone, Dr. J., and the rest of the 65-game-winning Sixers. It was also just another in a series of enormous events that would make the '80s the greatest decade of them all.

The ever-feisty Malone, who was the league MVP for the third time, began those playoffs with his famous, ballsy prediction of "Fo, Fo, Fo." He was almost right. The Sixers, riding the back of Malone along with Dr. J., Chicagoan Mo Cheeks, Celtic killer Andrew Toney, and sixth man Bobby Jones, would go 12-1, sweeping everyone except the Milwaukee Bucks, who'd beaten them in Game 4.

On the day before the Finals were to begin, I'd approached Moses in the locker room to ask a quick question. Mind you, I'd never had a single dealing with him at any other time, including the games with the Bulls. I'd always stuck with Erving and Cheeks, both of whom were easy to deal with.

I had gotten within about five feet of Malone when he looked up and saw me coming. "I ain't got nothin' to say to you motherfucker," he said, his eyes zeroing in on me like a fighter pilot. I wanted to tell him that he must be mistaking me for someone else, but I didn't see any point in wasting my breath. I'd already been told that Moses was a difficult dude most of the time, anyway. And it was also possible that Moses didn't want to deal with any motherfucker. I just happened to be the one closest to him.

As it turned out, this would be the only NBA championship of Dr. J's storied career, so he was the better story. Certainly a more cooperative subject. He spent more than an hour after Game 4 answering the same questions over and over with patience and class.

For most of the '80s, Magic Johnson's Lakers and Larry Bird's Celtics would become involved in what many consider the NBA's greatest rivalry, consistently producing amazing Finals that carried on a rivalry that began in the 1979 NCAA title game when Johnson's Michigan State team beat Bird and his upstart Indiana State team. That would change in 1989 when the Pond Scum Detroit Pistons would take their turn atop the NBA, but that was only after Bird's balky back slowed him to a crawl.

There was also this little NBA thing in '80s involving someone named Michael Jordan, who torched that very same Celtics dynasty for an NBA playoff-record 63 points (breaking the mark of 61 set by Elgin Baylor) at Boston Garden in Game 2 of the Eastern Conference quarterfinals in 1986. In one of the most unbelievable sequences in a completely surreal game, Jordan took the ball to the basket where he was met by the Hall of Fame trio of Bird, Robert Parish, and Kevin McHale at the rim. Considered by many to be the best frontcourt in NBA history, Jordan appeared to still be going up while the three HOFs were on the way down. And he scored.

That the Bulls would lose in two overtimes mattered not. It all led to Bird calling Jordan the greatest player he'd ever seen, noting, "It's just God disguised as Michael Jordan."

Jordan had already made his imprint on the college side, hitting the game-winning shot from the wing as North Carolina beat Georgetown and coach John Thompson in the '82 NCAA championship game. Even at the early point, the surly Thompson was well on his way to becoming one of the biggest asswipes of the decade. More about that later.

And much of that decade produced remarkable championship games, including Jim Valvano and North Carolina State in '83, Villanova's startling upset of Georgetown and Thompson (still an asswipe) in 1985, Larry Brown and Kansas beating Big Eight rival Oklahoma in 1988, and my old buddy Steve Fisher taking Michigan to an 80-79 win over Seton Hall in '89.

That Michigan team, by the way, lost twice to a great Illinois team during the course of the regular season, including a blowout loss to the Illini in the last game of the regular season in Ann Arbor. The Wolverines exacted their revenge in the semifinals with a win over Illinois on a putback basket by Sean Higgins. And I can guarantee you to this very day that Nick Anderson thinks Higgins pushed him out of the way to get the ball. And Anderson was right.

My streak would run to covering five straight NCAA championship games before I left the *Sun-Times*. The last was Duke's victory over Kansas in 1991, the year in which UNLV would come oh-so-close to a perfect season, and perhaps earning support as the best team of all-time.

And at this point, that's just a teaser, a small sampling of the glorious '80s, when Hall & Oates were riding high on the pop charts and I was hauling ass around the world after becoming a *Sun-Times* columnist in 1988.

It's always been insisted by many who know the game best that the NFL is a better place when the Bears are contenders. I believe John Madden said that more than once, but it's all a little fuzzy these days.

The Bears have been an afterthought for much of this century, making just their second Super Bowl in 2006. That was a terrific trip for The Score, but not so much for the Bears, who lost to Peyton Manning and the Indianapolis Colts. Since then, their record has been stuck on one win in the 51 Super Bowls played to date. A heritage franchise, yes. A good franchise? Not really.

No wonder the '85 Bears sparked such a love affair, which began not long after they lost the 1984 title game to the San Francisco 49ers 23-0. But you just knew that despite that result, the Bears would be back with a vengeance the next season and they were.

Called by many the most colorful cast of characters in NFL history, the Bears and their defense roared through the '85 season, losing just once to the Miami Dolphins in a Monday night game. Fridge Perry, Mongo McMichael, Mike Singletary, Otis Wilson, the Punky QB, Richard Dent, Wilber Marshall, Gary Fencik, and others all became (and remain) mythical figures, eating up opponents and getting plenty of attention, none more so than the gum-chewing, lip-flapping Ditka.

Meanwhile, defensive coordinator Buddy Ryan was being given almost as much of the credit for his 46 defense, which continually mashed the opposition into a fine mist.

Their 46-10 win over a not-so-good New England team would forever have some insisting the Bears were the greatest team of all-time. Make that the greatest single-season team of all-time. That Bears bunch would never see the Super Bowl again, sustaining a series of playoff losses in the years that followed that were both puzzling and disconcerting.

Yes, McMahon's health was a constant headache. But I've always kind of figured that Ditka, despite all the glory coming his way, should have been more harshly criticized (just another reason we didn't get along) when he told his players to knock off all the endorsement deals and concentrate on football.

This from a guy who'd sell snow to an Alaskan. He never stopped his personal gravy train, making him a do as I say guy, not a do as I do guy. Am I saying he was do-do? Yes. A hypocrite? Most definitely. What right did he have to tell grown-ass men not to make side money, while he rolled in it?

Did any of that lead to the Bears' inability to make a return trip to the Super Bowl? Maybe. Maybe not. But it left a bad taste in plenty of mouths, as did his tough-guy act, which never grew old with the people who loved him.

But even as Ditka's Bears battled to get back over the Super Bowl hump, Jordan's battles became much more interesting, especially on a national level after his eruption in the 1986 play-offs vs. Boston.

I can attest that Jordan's arrival in Chicago was rather understated. It just didn't seem like many people cared, perhaps because it was a Bears town or maybe it was because the Cubs had a red-hot summer and a division championship that would eventually lead to the heartbreak of San Diego.

Here's what I knew: the guy had an NCAA championship under his belt as well as a shiny gold medal for Team USA's victory at the '84 Summer Olympics.

And in the early part of fall in 1984, he was waiting for me at the old "Purple Palace," aka the Lincolnwood Hyatt. Tucked at the corner of Lincoln and Touhy, the PP was the headquarters for Bulls coaches, veterans, and rookies alike during training camp.

I can't say I knew I was going to meet basketball's GOAT for our first one-on-one interview, but I was certainly a helluva lot more excited than most Chicagoans.

The Jordan then could not be compared to the billionaire we see today. He was just a kid from Wilmington, North Carolina, then, still chasing his dream. He even said to me, "I never saw a purple building before," when I asked what he thought of the hotel.

As for the camp itself, Jordan was surprised by one thing. "Professional players can sit down during practices," Jordan said. "You never, ever sat down in one of Dean [Smith's] practices and you sure never sat during one of Bobby [Knight's]."

That first day of camp was "kind of lonely" according to coach Kevin Loughery.

By Day 2, Jordan had begun to assert himself and Loughery had already started to scheme for an offense that would get the ball to the rookie as much as possible. In all fairness, Loughery, a veteran of many NBA wars, knew it after the first day.

He was coming off the court and he had this strange expression on his face, sort of a mix of wonderment with a hint of "am I crazy." "I just saw the greatest basketball player I've ever seen," Loughery said that day. "I'm not kidding."

Now, NBA coaches who've been around the block a few times might be prone to say some odd things at times, but this wasn't one of those occasions.

Loughery meant it. He also was right.

I don't think he was right later in camp when he said rather than Julius Erving, he would compare Jordan to Jerry West. See, coaches do say the darndest things.

Jordan was a practice terror just about every step of the way, but early on it was Quintin Dailey who decided he was going to make him pay for it. While not necessarily known for his defense, Dailey had begun to assert himself, doing a slow bump and grind with Jordan, never taking a backward step.

During a break that day, Dailey walked to the edge of the court. "Michael's great," Dailey said to me. "But don't tell him I said that."

I didn't, but the supposed secret of Jordan didn't last much longer.

You might remember guard Dirk Minniefield, who'd played at Kentucky and whose best friend in the world was Sam Bowie. See where I'm going.

By Day 6 of the camp, Minniefield admitted to being awestruck. "Michael is unbelievable," Minniefield said. "Houston and Portland are both going to be sorry they didn't draft him. The thing is, he keeps getting better every day. If he keeps doing that he'll be Superman. Wait, he already is Superman."

Bowie, beset by continuing leg injuries, was a titanic bust at No. 2. No. 1 pick Hakeem Olajuwon did win two titles for the Rockets, but both came when Jordan was playing baseball. Would those Rockets teams have beaten the Bulls with Jordan? Nobody else ever did in the NBA Finals, so the answer is no.

We know that Jordan's journey to the top wasn't easy, that it took a few stumbles along the way, but that doesn't mean he wasn't one of the biggest stars of the decade. He was all that and more.

But let's get to a few other guys who also helped make the '80s the most memorable decade of them all.

I HAD FLOWN into Tampa, Florida, in early March of 1988, rented a car at the airport, and made a beeline for Plant City, which was then the spring training home of the Cincinnati Reds and manager Pete Rose.

At this point, Rose wasn't player-manager anymore, just manager. He'd been the Reds' player-manager on Sept. 11, 1985, when he got the 4,193rd hit of his career off San Diego pitcher Eric Show, reaching a milestone that had seemed untouchable for decades, a record many had insisted would never be broken.

When I finally got to the facility about an hour before the game, Rose was holding court with a few of his players along the third-base line, demonstrating what appeared to be the proper position to field a grounder. I remember thinking that if the kids on the team didn't know that by then, there was no hope for any of us.

It's just as possible Rose was simply messing around, telling some story under the guise of instruction.

By the time he was done, the media was being told to beat it, that the field needed to be gussied up for first pitch. At that point I was mad for running about a half-hour late in getting to the park, but there was nothing I could do about a slight travel delay.

The game with the Phillies wasn't all that interesting, either, but the day was warm and beautiful, just what any snowbird would want.

I was already poised behind home plate as the final out of the game was recorded. I'd been told that Rose would conduct his postgame press conference on the field.

I let the game and player questions pass, just staying out of the way. There really wasn't much to it. After the writers and radio guys had left, Rose, who'd been sitting in the dugout, started to get up, but I was on him.

I introduced myself and asked if he had a few minutes. Although he'd appeared ready to call it a day, Rose said, "Sure. What do you need?"

And for the next two hours, Rose stayed in that exact same place. He talked about his dad, his upbringing, the Big Red Machine of the '70s, the art of hitting, his collision with Ray Fosse at the 1970 All-Star Game (no regrets), his hit record, and what it meant to be managing the Reds. "Love it," he said. "I just fucking love it."

I had a great start for a book, let alone a simple column. Rose even told me he'd enjoyed the conversation. That was the only time that ever happened to me with someone of Rose's renown.

What happened to Rose about 18 months later would provide no one with a particularly happy postscript to what had been the most remarkable of decades. Baseball Commissioner Bart Giamatti announced on Aug. 24, 1989, that Rose would receive a lifetime suspension from baseball for betting on the game. In 1990, Rose was sentenced to five months in jail on tax charges.

And as we stand almost 20 years later, Rose doesn't appear as if he'll ever be back in baseball's good graces. His pleas were continually rejected by old Commissioner Bud Selig, and Selig's successor Rob Manfred made it pretty clear that Rose would remain on the outside looking in. And he'll stay there. Adding to his already tarnished legend were the revelations of him having sex with a 16-year-old girl. I suddenly feel dirty for having spent so much time with this creep.

Rose had actually carved himself out a decent set of grades for his work in the 2016 World Series for Fox, but that network whacked him after the sex scandal. And I don't think I'll see him anytime soon on a baseball broadcast.

I still see Rose when we go for our yearly trip to Las Vegas. He makes what he claims to be a pretty good living signing all sorts of things at The Art of Music memorabilia store located in the walkway between the Luxor and Mandalay Bay.

The last time I saw him was in the winter of 2015. He had a four-hour signing at the store, then headed over to the Mandalay Bay sports book. And how do I know this? Because I was betting horses when Rose and a friend plopped down about 20 feet away from where I was sitting. I didn't approach him, didn't say a thing even after his friend had left. For his part, Rose never budged, never placed a bet, just stared blankly ahead at the giant-screen TVs for about 90 minutes.

He looked sad, even disconsolate at times. I don't know what he was thinking, or if he was even thinking anything. There's also a chance that I was reading too much into the entire thing.

Maybe I was. But I still believe to this day that I know one of those 1,000-yard stares when I see one. You know, the limp, blank unfocused gaze generally associated with a battle-weary soldier.

Again, I'm not trying to associate Rose with PTSD in respect for our men and women in the military. I just know that whatever it was that day, Rose didn't seem to be himself. Maybe it was just an upset stomach or maybe he was used to having people run bets for him, which I'd seen happen in the '90s when we'd do radio shows from Vegas.

I do know that if your most fervent wish was to see Rose suffer for his misdeeds, or perhaps, you just dislike him in general, that afternoon would have probably made you very happy.

THE LAST OF my sit-downs with one of the biggest sports news-makers of the '80s came about quite unexpectedly on just about every level.

I was sitting in the bleachers at the 1988 Olympic Trials, which were being held at the IU Michael A. Carroll Track & Soccer Stadium in Indianapolis. The dates were July 15-23, which meant two things. I was doing my homework for the upcoming Summer Olympics in Seoul and sweating my ass off.

It must have been 105 degrees that day and I had no covering. I also didn't have much of a clue what I was watching, but remember, columnists are supposed to know everything. Just ask one.

So there I was, not accomplishing much of anything. I could have stayed in my hotel room, which I'd made sure was icy cold and just waited for the results to come my way without getting into such a lather.

That's when I glanced to my left and noticed a solitary figure sitting there, gazing intently at the track. It was Carl Lewis.

I don't think I'd covered any kind of track meet in probably 15 years, but I knew at best Lewis had a prickly relationship with the media, that he wasn't all that interested in sharing. He was called "vain, shallow, and self-absorbed" by Richard Moore, author of *The Dirtiest Race in History*, and those words were probably on the kind side.

I remember a buddy of mine had warned me that Lewis was a complete jerkoff, that he was above it all.

But I got up and sidled toward him that day, figuring the worst thing that could happen was that Lewis would tell me to go fuck myself. Hey, that wouldn't be the first time.

I asked Lewis if I could sit next to him. "Go ahead," he said, even making quick eye contact.

So there I was, sitting beside a guy who would soon become one of the most decorated athletes in track history, claiming a total of eight Olympic gold medals, a silver Olympic medal, and 10 World Championship medals.

"I bet you want to talk about fucking Ben Johnson," Lewis said. Yes, I said, let's talk about fucking Ben Johnson, who'd gone from a stick-figure of a kid to a finely muscled machine by the mid-'80s. An eye-opener, indeed.

Lewis was one of the medal kings at the '84 L.A. Olympics, expecting to capture plenty of lucrative endorsement deals along the way. He did his part by winning, but as it turned out the folks from Madison Ave. were just not interested. Seems that Lewis had done little to engender much goodwill at the '84 Games, not only with fans, but in the eyes of teammates, who didn't appreciate the fact he had not stayed at the Olympic Village.

"I've always done things my way," Lewis said of the lingering ill-will. Normally, I would have loved to play devil's advocate in those situations, but that's not what I was looking to accomplish.

I was digging for much different dirt.

The Lewis-Johnson battle royale began to bloom in 1985, the first year in which Lewis had lost a 100-meter race to the Canadian in Zurich.

Johnson would put together a string of four consecutive wins over Lewis, including a narrow victory at the World Championships at Rome in 1987. The two reportedly had to be separated after that race, a sure sign that the two were at the "I hate your guts" stage. And they would stay there.

Unlike others in sports we've all seen since then, Lewis wasn't afraid to call Johnson out, making him rather unique, considering we would be witness to an entire generation of baseball players who didn't know nothing from nothing about any steroid abuse.

"He [Johnson] cannot do what he does without drugs," Lewis said that day, his voice taking on a sharp edge.

What I didn't know at the time because it wouldn't become public until 2003 was that Lewis had failed three drug tests of his own at those very trials, testing positive for three banned stimulants. The volume of those stimulants would not result in a ban under today's guidelines, but at the time it would have been enough to get him kicked off the team.

The Americans eventually managed to clear him on appeal, but I can never imagine what the '88 Olympics would have been like without him.

Now, I'll never know for sure if Lewis knew that very day we talked that he had tested positive, but if he did, he deserves an Academy Award. His outrage was palpable, his words were sharp and to the point. It's just that in the murky world of track and field you're never sure what's real.

IF YOU'RE STILL skeptical about my claim about the '80s, allow me to add even more highlights.

For most of us who had to deal with Bill Buckner at any point, the ground ball that went between his legs and cost the Red Sox the World Series in 1986 was sweet. The only downside was the Mets won.

Is there any sports image in history that's better than the Stanford band on the field as Cal returned a kickoff for the game-winning touchdown as time expired in the 1982 classic? I didn't think so.

Kirk Gibson's homer off the virtually unhittable Dennis Eckersley of Oakland to win the first game of the 1988 World Series for the Dodgers. Gibson was another jerk. But give him his due on this one. A truly iconic moment.

Doug Flutie's Hail Mary pass to Gerard Phalen to beat Miami 47-45 in 1984. Flutie would win the Heisman Trophy that year, but this pass had nothing to do with it. The votes had already been counted.

Jack Nicklaus wins '86 Masters at the age of 46. A truly remarkable achievement for the Golden Bear. The only downside were the pants he was wearing. Wait, I had a pair just like those.

George Brett went out of his damn-fool mind after being called out for having too much pine tar on his bat during a game with the Yankees on July 24, 1983. We should all be so lucky. The beauty of Brett is that he still hates the Yankees to this very day, never letting go of the seething rivalry that was built as the two teams battled for American League supremacy.

Sugar Ray Leonard, in a rematch that came just five months after he'd lost the WBC welterweight title to Roberto Duran, caused Duran to say perhaps the two most famous words in boxing history—"No Más!"

Cubs manager Lee Elia went off the charts with a postgame rant aimed at Cubs fans on April 29, 1983. If you haven't heard it, find it. Top that, Joe Maddon.

Holy terror Mike Tyson knocks out Michael Spinks in 31 seconds to claim the heavyweight championship in Atlantic City. Not one of my proudest moments. I'd picked the then-undefeated Spinks. Shit.

Lord knows we've seen plenty of college basketball upsets over the years, but No. 1 Virginia's 77-72 loss in 1982 to Chaminade, an NAIA school at the time with a recruiting budget of $34, still remains near the top. The day before Chaminade had lost to Wayland Baptist. Waylon Jennings should have written a song.

Roger Clemens strikes out 20 Mariners in 1986, a record that was equaled by the Cubs' Kerry Wood in 1998. Wood's game ranks as the best pitched game in major league history according to Game Score.

The Year of 1981 became the year of Fernandomania in Los Angeles. The soft-spoken Valenzuela became an icon in just one season, throwing five shutouts in his first seven starts, which were all complete games.

I could never get enough of the easily irritated, bug-eyed John McEnroe and he came through for me big-time at Wimbledon in 1981, screaming "You cannot be serious" at the chair umpire. Classic.

My personal favorite was Willie Shoemaker's victory with Ferdinand in the 1986 Kentucky Derby. Starting from the rail position, the 17-1 shot was dead last after a half-mile, stuck behind a virtual wall of horses. But then the 54-year-old Shoemaker somehow found a path up the rail and closed like a freight train to win going away by a stunning 2½ lengths, only adding to his legend and becoming the oldest jockey to ever win the Derby. I was standing at the wire that day, and I'll never forget the prolonged ovation Shoemaker got from the monster crowd as he brought Ferdinand back around to the front stretch. It gave me goosebumps that day. And when I think about it, it still does.

BUT AS PURE as my love is for so many sports moments, so too is my pure hatred for two men and one team I had the misfortune to deal with on many occasions in the '80s…and for that I am eternally sorry.

Let's start with easily the most loathsome bastard of them all, former Indiana basketball coach Bob Knight, the red-sweater-wearing prick who not very long ago hoped that every Indiana University official who had something to do with his firing in 2000 was dead.

This from the guy who didn't know (or care) about the fine line between coaching players and abusing them. There are all sorts of tapes and videos that have surfaced over the years, but I don't need any of them to draw an accurate portrayal of Knight, who won three national championships in his 29 years at IU, the last coming in 1987 when Indiana beat Syracuse on a last-second shot by Keith Smart. I covered that game for the *Sun-Times*. It still makes me sick, even though Syracuse coach Jim Boeheim is another five-alarm asshole.

That was Knight's final high point as a college coach. He had no great moments as a broadcaster after ESPN surprised a lot of people by hiring him to analyze college buckets in 2008. That was quite a choice by Knight, given the fact that he once called basketball media work "one or two steps above prostitution." As most expected, he'd flamed out coaching at Texas Tech, leaving the job to his son, Pat, who was later called a loser and a bully by Deadspin.

Shocking, eh?

Here's another. Knight and I actually had one cordial conversation in 1986 after John Feinstein's master work *A Season on the Brink* came out. His usual blusterous and angry self that long ago day, Knight had plenty of venom he directed toward Feinstein, whose book chronicled the Hoosiers' 1985-86 season. I remember Knight feeling betrayed that he'd given Feinstein complete access only to get a rather unflattering result. Duh.

Knight's comments to me made some national news the next few days, but I was only a conduit for his vile feelings. I don't recall us ever exchanging another civil word and that's fine with me. I never had one for him.

We spend a lot of time these days worrying about the bullying that happens around us, whether it be at work or school or a playground, wherever. I'm hoping the majority of us would like to see it stopped, period. But it's clear that will probably never happen, no matter what we do.

Even our current President of the United States had no trouble trotting out Knight and Mike Ditka, another bully, to back his campaign. To paraphrase, both of the fuck-faced fossils were his kind of guys—winners. Barf bag, please.

Knight's final day of work on ESPN came at the 2015 NIT Championship game between Miami and Stanford at Madison Square Garden, which garnered about as much attention as a pie-eating contest.

There was nothing memorable about that broadcast that I could find. I don't even know if Knight was awake for it. Just like Ditka, there was a rumor that he'd once been caught sleeping on the set. I like him better asleep.

The other guy I hate with an all-abiding passion is yet another former college basketball coach, John Thompson, who also became a member of the media after years of being about as anti-media as you can possibly get.

Thompson wore out the Us vs. The World mantra in the first five minutes at Georgetown, but that never stopped him from droning on and on and on as the years rolled past. He would eventually become the first African-American coach to win a major collegiate championship when his '84 Hoyas won the NCAA title.

He was also known for keeping his players away from the media at just about any cost, allowing you to formulate whatever opinions you had on your own. Not that I wanted to know more about a guy like Michael Graham, one of the dirtiest players I've ever seen.

One of the many he didn't do any favors for with the media ban was Patrick Ewing, who wasn't the glowering, angry guy everyone kind of believed he was. Now the new Georgetown coach, turns out Ewing was often very thoughtful and very approachable in his days with the Knicks. He had something to say, even in the most difficult of times. I just wish I'd known that sooner.

But all of Thompson's bullshit at Georgetown was just a warmup for his stint as the 1988 U.S. Olympic basketball coach in Seoul, South Korea.

Apparently believing that it said Georgetown on their uniforms instead of USA, Thompson stayed true to form when he announced through one of the Olympic lackeys that there would be no media access to the United States team, noting that practices would be closed and players would not be available. (NBA players would be for brief times.) The only press conference would be after the game. The publicist called it "virtual non-existent access."

Such a screaming turd. Thompson was allowed by idiot Olympic officials to throw his considerable weight around, to do as he pleased, just as he always did.

How mad was the American press corps? Mad enough to openly cheer for the Soviet Union team in the semifinals, which I'm pretty sure was a first. That Russia won was doubly pleasing to me and most others. Watching Thompson squirm after the game was great fun, as was writing about the loss. I was glad jerks don't always win.

The last name on my hit list for the '80s are the Detroit Pistons, aka The Bad Boys, aka the filthiest basketball just about anyone had ever seen.

Long before they would win the first of their back-to-back championships in 1989, they had taken special delight in attacking Michael Jordan, and this was long before the Bulls grew into a title contender.

Remorseless slug Bill Laimbeer took to knocking Jordan out of the air at least once a game, or so it seemed. And it was never done legally. Laimbeer didn't care. Neither did Rick Mahorn, another guy who was only too happy to undercut people anytime, anywhere. And I haven't mentioned the irritation caused by Dennis Rodman, who later become a beloved member of the Bulls. Never beloved by me, however. And I don't want to forget Isiah Thomas, who was the main culprit during the infamous 1985 All-Star Game freeze out of Michael Jordan, a story I broke along with Thomas Bonk of the *Los Angeles Times*.

I understand that intimidation is part of the game, but too many of those Pistons went well beyond that, not giving a fuck who they left in their wake. I'm glad their reign was relatively short and the Bulls ultimately left them scurrying for the locker room after eliminating them in 1991.

So what did I enjoy more: the Soviet Union beating the United States or the Bulls beating the Pistons?

We'll call it a tie.

chapter 18

My Toughest Assignment

I've covered some of the biggest sporting events on our planet, including the '88 Olympics in Seoul, several NBA Finals, baseball playoffs galore, NCAA championship basketball games, almost a decade of Kentucky Derbies, NBA playoffs from start to finish, Rose Bowls, and just about anything else you can think of. Hell, I had all of 35 minutes to write the final edition game story for the *Chicago Sun-Times* after the Bulls beat the Lakers for their first championship in 1991.

Most of that I did efficiently (if you don't count that crazy first story back in 1979 when I nearly blew it) and effectively, learning how to fly on the fly. That's the nature of newspapers. Move it or lose it.

Then I came to what I figured would take up two chapters in this very book. I'd been warned that writing about your own illness can be difficult, that recounting so many unpleasant memories wouldn't be easy.

I didn't believe that for a second. I wrote professionally for 20 years and I thought I knew myself well enough to recount anything, no matter how unpleasant.

I was wrong. Again.

I struggled with these next two chapters way more than I should have, certainly way more than I thought possible. Sometimes writing isn't just writing, even if you're dealing with a set of facts that can't be altered. Sometimes, writing can seem like torture. The late, great Red Smith famously said when asked if churning out a daily column was a chore, "Why no. You simply sit down at a typewriter, open your veins and bleed."

Spoken like a true red-blooded American.

So here goes.

I'VE SPENT COUNTLESS HOURS over the years reading gut-wrenching, tear-inducing tales about athletes and others who've fought cancer with every part of their being. Football players, baseball players, stock-car drivers, musicians, people from all walks of life. No one is immune. Some of them won the ultimate battle. Many more did not.

And, as noted earlier, I've experienced both sides up close, first through my mother and then my oldest son, John, giving me a perspective that can be uplifting at times, but frankly remains downright terrifying no matter what.

Chances are you've lost a loved one to cancer. You probably remember relying on hope and prayer coupled with the wonders of modern medicine, clinging for days, months, and maybe even years as you watched that person waste away.

On vacation with Carolyn outside Vienna in summer 2014.

My story began innocently enough. It was the first week of May 2014. I was driving home from one of our Budweiser Who Needs Two Tavern Tour remotes, when I was suddenly hit with a sharp, painful feeling on the left side of my jaw. I was tempted to pull the car over and collect myself, but Friday night rush hours can be unforgiving. I wasn't sure I'd even be able to get back on the road, so I pressed on.

My plan was simple. If it continued to ache the next day, I would seek help.

Of course, it persisted. I made the call to my dentist, who was out of town. I didn't want to wait, so I called my wife's dentist. They shoehorned me in on Monday, probably because I described the pain as an eight out of 10, which is basically intolerable.

We exchanged our usual pleasantries that Monday. He was a fan of the show and never lacked a kind word. He didn't spend more than a minute or so looking in my mouth before telling me that I needed to see an oral surgeon, telling me there was a cyst in the gum line.

Doesn't sound bad, right? But it was.

I made the appointment to see the oral surgeon for the late morning of May 15, a scant two days before we were scheduled to take our first trip to Europe. I kept hoping the pain would dissipate. No such luck.

By the time May 15 rolled around, I had gotten that certain sense of dread one gets when long-anticipated plans might have to be altered. After all, we had booked this Paris trip more than a year earlier and had built plenty of anticipation in the meantime.

The surgeon told me in no uncertain terms that the cyst needed to come out and it needed to come out right damn now. Not much you say to that other than go ahead.

The procedure probably took about 30 minutes or so. It just seemed longer.

When he was done, I asked if he thought I could still make the trip. He said he would supply me with some pain meds, carefully noting that flying in a pressurized cabin for nine hours or so wouldn't be recommended for recovery, adding, "But I won't stop you. Just depends on your pain tolerance." Fair enough.

He also told me my mouth would take roughly 18 months to heal properly, and that I should be aware the cyst could return.

I conveniently put that out of my mind, at least for the short run.

Just as I thought it would be, the trip was spectacular. The French weren't anywhere as snooty as many had warned, and the three-hour bus trip from Rouen to Omaha Beach was every bit as great as I had hoped. You can't walk that beach, but you can get close enough to feel the history.

Better yet, aside from the first day or so, I wasn't in pain.

By the time I saw the surgeon 15 months later, we had been on another European cruise and I was feeling like I had dodged a bullet.

Turns out I hadn't.

As the 18-month date rolled around, I had this nagging feeling that something was wrong. It was. The cyst had come back and yet another surgery date needed to be set.

This time, perhaps only in my imagination, the surgery seemed to hurt twice as much. Even worse, the doctor said he was going to put a drain in the opening to speed up the healing.

That proved to be a disaster. The drain wouldn't stay where it was supposed to, eventually coming out for good about a week later after absolutely driving me out of my mind.

I didn't miss a single day of work during all of this, refusing to believe that this was going to get the best of me, living up to that work ethic my father had preached to me so many years ago when I was scrubbing those milk trucks.

Little did I know the worst was yet to come, that the most evil of all enemies was just laying in the weeks, waiting to reveal its ugly head.

chapter 19

Cancer

By the time 2016 began, I had already made up my mind that I was going to retire on Jan. 2, 2017, giving me exactly 25 years at The Score.

There was no one reason for that decision, just a culmination of things, mostly realizing that if I ever was going to enjoy life to the absolute fullest in the time I had left, work could no longer be part of it. And yes, most days I was broadcasting from my home studio, which had traveled with me from Mokena to Orland Park when we moved in October 2014.

That perk was something I had long ago negotiated, understanding the cash might not always be there. Now don't get me wrong. Cash is good, but there's nothing wrong with getting a few things that will make the day-to-day grind more comfortable. Besides, there's nothing better than having the amazing Dave Miska at your house, mapping out just the right battle plan. Installing the ISDN line is the easy part. Making sure the acoustics of the room are perfect is far more important.

Dave told my brother-in-law Michael Harper what he needed done to the room and Michael took care of it. And, of course, it turned out perfect.

All I needed to discuss with Mitch was when he wanted to run my farewell column, which would be posted on The Score's website. I could have just done it on the air, but the old writer in me wanted to do it with a column first.

Mitch left the time open, just telling me to write the goodbye piece and they'd have it for whenever. Not a problem. But then nothing was ever a problem too big for Rosen, who'd become The Score's GM in 2005 and would later also become the GM for our friends at WXRT.

About the only thing that Mitch couldn't quite overcome was getting Danny Mac to feel like working, because there were times when he just didn't want to. Those were days when Mitch would

I made it back on air in December 2016, and we did the final Boers and Bernstein Show at Real Time Sports in Elk Grove Village.
(Courtesy of 670 The Score)

have to haul ass to Indiana to see Danny face to face. It didn't work, despite their longtime friendship. Danny and Matt Spiegel, who had produced our show years back, had established a nice niche for themselves in the midday spot, and our transitions with them were generally fun.

Danny would eventually leave the station for a second time, taking what would turn out to be a relatively short morning-show run on The Drive with co-host Pete McMurray. He exited in early June of 2016, just 16 months into a three-year deal.

What set Danny off this time was that The Drive bosses told him not to discuss on the air the firing of his longtime friend Greg Solk, who'd been pushed out the door despite the fact he was the guy who'd put The Drive together.

Not long after that hallway scene, Danny was out of work, although The Drive paid Danny for the rest of his contract.

Little did I know that as my friend was unraveling again, I would soon begin what was to become the hardest health year of my life, a year that continues to leave me with self-doubt, not to mention a healthy dose of worry about my own mortality.

Such thoughts went racing through my mind when the cyst reappeared for the third time in the early part of April. Something just wasn't right.

This time the oral surgeon wanted no part of it, referring me instead to a specialist in Homer Glen. I had one appointment with him during which he described the surgery, which included replacing my jawbone with my fibula, a process that immediately left me with way more questions than there were answers. The most obvious being, would I ever be able to walk normally again.

Yes, I would be able to, he answered. A relief. But he cautioned that this would not be easy no matter what, that the recovery time was generally long and painful, and there's always the possibility that such difficult surgery could lead to other complications.

I appreciated the honesty. He told me he would be in touch when he had more details.

At no time, however, did he ever mention cancer. I felt shaken and relieved at the same time, if that's even possible.

A few days later he called back, saying he wanted me and my wife to come in at 10 AM on a Saturday. "It's not an appointment," he said. "I just need to tell you guys some things."

What he told us was that he was transferring my case to Northwestern Hospital, noting they were much better prepared to handle my particular needs, including the name of the specialist who would be performing the surgery.

That made sense. Northwestern has long been on the cutting edge of many medical procedures (if you'll pardon the expression), so there was no alarm on my part, only getting to Northwestern in the early morning was a hassle, particularly for the half-dozen or so appointments I needed.

It also left me without much prep time for the show those days, but I did the best I could to be ready at 1 PM. Even at that, I felt like I was cheating the listeners. But as it turned out, it didn't manifest itself in any noticeable manner, at least not as far as I could tell. I met my surgeons, Dr. Urjeet Patel and Dr. Sandeep Samant. Only later would I learn that Dr. Patel generally did not perform the surgery unless there had been cancer detected, which was not the case with me up to that point. I also loved it that no one from his office had any idea who I was or what I did. I've come over the years to enjoy a certain anonymity, although it has gotten progressively tougher and tougher.

I made it through the various tests, consultations, and whatever else they wanted me to do, ultimately reaching the point where the surgery date was set for June 16, 2016.

I made it public knowledge on the show a few days before the 16th that I would be MIA for a while. To be honest, I've never gotten completely comfortable with sharing such information, but in this case there was no getting around it.

If you're in the public spotlight in any way, you have to be willing to share. Don't make people guess, don't have someone else do it (unless absolutely necessary), and for the love of God don't lie.

In today's social media crazed society, the last thing you want to do is open the floodgates to Twitter hell.

So Boers is gone, huh? What is it? Drug rehab? Gambling rehab? Domestic abuse? Caught dog fighting? Molesting one of his make-believe monkeys?

Hey, anything is possible in the imagination of those who are so inclined. Being forthright remains the best policy until somebody proves we have all shifted to the Fake News format.

The one thing I didn't have was a time frame. Here's what I knew: the surgery would be anywhere from 10-15 hours in duration, that I would probably spend at least three days in the ICU, and the total length of the hospital stay would be dictated by circumstances.

As it turned out, the two givens were indeed fairly accurate, not bad considering nothing is for certain in any surgical procedure.

What I wasn't expecting was that they'd found a metastasized cancerous tumor on my jawbone. It was gone, of course, with the new bone set in place, but the long-term treatment plan had been altered.

Now it would be several rounds of chemotherapy and 30 doses of radiation on the left side of my face, which would probably start sometime in early August.

My hopes of returning to The Score in a timely fashion were suddenly gone. Little did I know how truly awful it would soon become.

I WOUND UP spending 15 days in the hospital, during which my anxiety ran at an all-time high roughly 99 percent of the time. Being penned in will do that to you. As will being unable to move without feeling excruciating pain in my jaw (it looked like I had a grapefruit stuck in the left side of my face). And my left leg didn't seem to want to do anything. But that was hardly unexpected. Just part of the spa package.

What I didn't know from the beginning was that before I could be sprung, I had to do two things. First, I needed to walk, even if aided by a cane. That cane thing was never going to happen. I could never quite get the rhythm down, so I abandoned it and worked harder to walk on my own. Second, I needed to be able to go up and down a flight of stairs with no help, something I was finally able to accomplish on Day 13.

For that I give credit to my physical therapist, who wouldn't take no for an answer no matter how many times I didn't feel like getting out of bed. I thank him for that, considering I can be as hard-headed as they come when the mood strikes, not to mention a big baby when in pain.

There was, however, one night that I will forever cherish during those interminable days. And, of course, it was sports-related. Surrounded by several family members, I had watched Game 7 of the NBA Finals between Cleveland and Golden State. Little did I know that very same thing would reoccur months later when it came time for the epic Game 7 of the World Series between the Cubs and Indians.

But as comforting as those nights were, I'd already experienced something that I simply cannot explain. And something that I've never told anyone—until now.

It happened on the second night after I'd been sprung from the ICU, a place where a sound sleep is almost impossible, considering you're being asked to wake up every few hours to check your vitals.

Maybe it was the sleep deprivation, maybe it was the pain meds, maybe it was a combination of the two. Not sure. What I am sure of is that I had never in my life had what can only be described as an out-of-my-fuckin-gourd experience.

It was in the wee hours of Saturday morning and I'd just been out of the ICU for slightly more than a day. That's when I started to get this weird feeling, as if I were suddenly floating on air. No matter how hard I tried I simply could not get my bearings. I didn't know what time it was, where I was, or what was happening. Kind of like a bad acid trip (or so I've been told).

I didn't know what part of the room I was in, let alone which room I was in. I didn't recognize a single thing.

The nurse came in a few moments later and wanted to know if I was okay, if she could get me anything. I told her I was fine, that L.A. never looked better to me.

"Alright," she said. "That must be some dream you're having."

But was it? Or was it just a hallucination, again territory that I hadn't explored since the late '60s? Gradually, I regained my senses, realizing that I was lying smack dab in the middle of the bed and that for the first time in days not feeling any pain. That didn't last long. Soon enough, everything ached again. I kind of liked where I'd been and I wanted to go back. No such luck. I was left dealing with the harsh reality of the many problems I had—and some that were yet to come.

I WAS ULTIMATELY released after 15 days in the hospital, but there was a catch. I was going home with a feeding tube and my wife would need a crash-course on how to use it.

And yes, I had a parade of occupational therapists and nurses who would come to our home in the weeks to come. But no one was going to come by three times a day and feed me.

Case closed.

That Carolyn readily picked it all up was a blessing because I needed to be fed that way for the next five weeks, leading up to the chemo and the radiation treatments, which were due to start in August.

I weighed 225 pounds before the surgery and 191 after, so any thought I had of putting any of the pounds back on was quickly dispelled. I was told I'd be lucky if I even maintained that much weight. I didn't. The stuff I was being fed was supposed to be high in this and high in that, but it looked more like baby formula and the longer it went on I started to forget what food even tasted like, which immediately reminded me of the old Three Stooges line, "Don't worry, it still tastes the same."

Gradually, you learn to cope because, frankly, there is no other viable choice. I hated every minute of it, even as I started to feel slightly better. Those five weeks dragged on seemingly forever, but I still harbored this sense of dread I couldn't shake. So yes, I am shamefully guilty of being a bad patient. But I've always been difficult no matter what the illness or injury.

Not something I'm proud of, mind you, but it's the truth.

As it turned out, my limits were yet to be truly tested.

Feeling a bit better, we moved into a small apartment on Lake St. when the radiation treatments began at the start of August. There's no way we could have made that trip every day for six weeks and stayed sane, so Northwestern hooks you up with a place to stay that's convenient and affordable. Well, kinda affordable.

Again, I had a steady stream of visitors from both The Score and my family, many of whom got the full benefit of the great rooftop view.

I didn't notice any immediate effects from the chemo, nor the radiation, but I knew what was to come. You can't get away from the inevitable. The radiation will get you in several ways. It did. For a time, my salivary glands stopped working. An awful feeling.

And the chemo was harsh, although at least it was a partial blessing to be rehydrated on those Tuesday afternoons.

At this point I was in complete limbo. I didn't feel terrible. I still had swelling on the left side of my face from the surgery and there was persistent pain, but I had this urge to go back to work.

It made no sense, really. Some days I was fine after the radiation, others I was hugging my pillow by 1 PM or so.

I never knew which it would be. I also had no idea what days I would actually feel hungry. I couldn't chew with the left side of my mouth, so eating anything but soft foods was out of the question.

I'd already taken on a skeletal look, so my desperation level rose even higher, but it's hard to force yourself to eat, so I made do on a steady diet of regular ice cream shakes and protein shakes, which were readily available downtown.

The only respite from the hotel-to-hospital-to-hotel routine came on Fridays when we'd take the train home after the 8:30 radiation treatment. That gave us the better part of three days in the comfort of home, but we were either taking the 6:15 AM train back to the city on Monday mornings or hitching a ride with our oldest son, John, who had an early start time for his job at Walsh Construction.

I pretty much ignored my 66th birthday on Sept. 13, saving it for exactly one week later when I had my 30th and final radiation treatment.

As a reward, the radiation department at Northwestern has a gong you can hit when you're at the end of Radiation Road. My recollection is that I hit the piss out of that gong. That's probably not true, given the fact I wasn't feeling particularly vital in any sense of the word. I was more Chuck Barris than Chuck Norris.

I thought I might be able to go back to work at that point, especially with the Cubs romping in the National League Central and the playoffs looming. It was pure folly. I never knew how I was going to feel from one hour to the next, let alone one day to the next. I'd already told Mitch that I was shooting to be back on Oct. 24, the day before the World Series was set to begin because I'd believed the Cubs would be in it.

Did I feel good? Absolutely not. The left side of my face remained swollen roughly three times its normal size because of what had been diagnosed as an infection 10 days or so into October. I had taken two full weeks of antibiotics by the time Oct. 24 rolled around, but it was clear the treatment hadn't worked.

But I had promised to return to the air and I did just that, quickly realizing I had made yet another error.

By the time week ended with the Bud Light Who Needs Tavern Tour at a bar in the Loop, I was feeling worse and worse, even though most of the shows were shortened for Cubs pregame. I was totally exhausted and in as much pain as I'd ever been in by the time we got out of the way at 5 PM.

I remember leaving, shaking hands with about 100 people who were welcoming me back. I love those people. But I knew my comeback, at least for then, was over.

On Halloween morning Carol and I grabbed the early train and headed for the Northwestern Emergency Room. I was eventually put into a regular room and surgery was scheduled for the next day, Tuesday, Nov. 1, to basically suck the infection out of my jaw. I felt as if I'd barged in to get what I needed, but there was no choice, this had to be done now in my world.

What I didn't realize was that I'd been basically sent back to square one again in terms of treatment. I'd be back on the feeding tube for the next six weeks. And for a special bonus, I had a Picc line put in my right arm for yet another six-week course of the most potent antibiotics man can muster. And who'd be doing all of it? Yep, Nurse Carol again.

But she did it all flawlessly, including the task of having to completely encase my right arm for the purposes of keeping it dry during a shower.

And as those six terrible weeks lurched along, I had in mind to try and return and get back in time for shows on the days leading up to Christmas. I also was preparing for my final show on Jan. 5, 2017. I wanted to make it the ultimate goodbye show, starting with the guys who'd been on the air when we opened for business on Jan. 2, 1992.

I made sure our longtime executive producer Matt Abbatacola got the list early. And, as always, he did a great job rounding up just about everyone I wanted, no easy task. More about that day in a bit.

Thankfully, I did make it back in December just before Christmas as Boers and Bernstein came to an end after more than 17 years on the air, a pretty damn good run by anyone's standards.

We did our last show as a team from Real Time Sports in Elk Grove Village, fitting because we'd done so many shows there over the years, plus we had several station events at the Belvidere Events and Banquet building adjacent to the bar.

All in all, it was a great day, albeit melancholy for obvious reasons. I was now down to one show, which was to be done from the soundstage on the ninth floor of the Prudential building. Talk about a perfect setting.

With the capacity to hold an audience, I was able to share that day with many of my family members, including two of my grandkids, Tyler and Josh, who were seated right in front of me.

I rarely over the years have rated any of the shows I've done, mainly because I tend to think I was probably bad. But not on this day.

We got all the original cast of the station. I will be eternally grateful that all the petty jealousies and hard feelings and whatever ill-will that might have remained was never in evidence. From Danny Mac to North to Shaer to Jiggetts to Hanley I can't thank them enough for that final stroll down memory lane. They were great.

My final show, A Toast to Terry Boers, aired on Jan. 5, 2017. It was a great day. *(Courtesy of 670 The Score)*

This was a celebration not as much for me as it was for everyone who'd persevered when we all went through the lean times, back to the days when I wasn't sure if we'd ever escape from the edge of the cliff where we often seemed to be perched.

It was great to catch up with so many people who'd meant so much to me, including Seth Mason, the man who hired me. When I asked him why he decided to hire me in the first place, Seth said he made it his point to find out who people thought was the funniest guy in the press box. I never knew that. But I got the job anyway.

There was only one other thing I wish I'd been able to do that last day—talk to the great Doug Buffone. One of my favorite guys of all-time, Doug and Ed O'Bradovich did the best damn postgame Bears show of anyone in this city's history. The two were passionate and fiery and fun and you never knew which direction they'd go next, especially when Doug brought out his so-called Neanderthal gene.

Doug, who died on April 20, 2015, just days after I had my shoulder replacement surgery, was truly a prince. And he was genuine. There wasn't a phony bone in his body and I loved him like the big brother I never had. And I always will.

That day belonged to him every bit as much as it did to me.

chapter 20

Thanks

So how did all this happen? Where did all this goodwill come from? How did I become the guy being called a radio legend? Flattering, sure. But based on what? Search me.

I still ask myself those questions these days and, no, I've never found a satisfactory answer because I don't think one exists.

I wasn't a prodigy when I was young, I didn't ace many classes in high school or college, and anyone who would have said I would be in the position I am today would have been accused of being high on crack, or at the very least under the influence of the demon rum. Or maybe both.

The guy who really nailed it was Gerry DiNardo. If I had a top 10 list of the people in America you should have dinner with, Gerry would be right near the top. A great storyteller, DiNardo is as genuine as it gets, warm, friendly, and perfectly real, something I wouldn't say about the majority of college coaches I've met over the years. They mainly fall into the category of ruthless, cold, and ultimately distrustful. Shake hands with many of them and you'll feel the need to be de-slimed. And once may not be enough.

Bernstein and I met with Gerry a few years back for the first of two evenings that were terrific fun. The former LSU and Indiana football coach turned star of the Big Ten Network said to me during our second dinner, "Don't be too hard on yourself, you've already won at life."

I must admit my shock. Geez, you'd think that a man of words would have heard that expression. I never had. But I accepted it, mainly because there's nothing pretentious about it in any way. But the career aside, I won the day the last of my four boys graduated from college, making it four-of-four. And how about the birth of my first grandchild in 2003 with four more to follow? That's winning, too. While this last year brought me a harsh sense of reality, it also brought me to the point where I know that no one who played a major part in my life should remain anonymous.

So if you can indulge me for a second here, I'd like to pass along thanks to people outside the newspaper and radio business who were instrumental in that win of a lifetime.

Let's start with Mary Pierce, my 8th grade English teacher at Steger Central Junior High. While I often took way too much delight in giving my teachers grief, a task I accelerated when I got to Bloom, Pierce was the very first teacher who ever indicated an appreciation for my writing.

It was in the weeks after the John F. Kennedy's assassination on Nov. 22, 1963, that she asked everyone in class to write something about JFK. No specifics were given, no road map. Just sit down and compose your thoughts. At 13, I wasn't sure I had any thoughts worth sharing, but I had thoughts.

I took the assignment seriously, something I didn't always do. I finally made up my mind to compare Kennedy's death with that of Abraham Lincoln. I can't tell you exactly what I wrote because

I couldn't find it anywhere. Here's what I do know. Pierce took the seven-paragraph essay and submitted it to something I think was called Interscholastic Magazine. And they printed it, making it my first byline.

Years later Pierce, at the asking of another former student of hers, would suddenly show up at one of our softball games at what used be called the Tinley Park Mental Health Center. Since I was already working on my second newspaper job at the time, I should have been thoughtful enough to tell her thanks, to give her credit where credit was due.

I remember we had a terrific conversation that night and I can recall her saying that she took a great delight in seeing her former students do well in life. It was, by far, the best conversation we ever had.

She had what appeared to be a hard exterior, but she was really a softie. I remember her as teacher, kind and willing to listen to a student, even if his explanation was nonsense. And believe me, I know or thing or two about nonsense.

I'm sure I frustrated her more than once as I did most of my teachers, but she didn't hold a grudge or write you off as a lost cause. She just tried harder.

The next lady I've mentioned in many different places over the years, including in the Arlington Heights *Daily Herald*.

Her name was Vera Kohloff, and by the time I took her creative writing course at Bloom High School in 1967, she was already in her 23rd year of teaching, having started at the school in 1944.

At that point, aside from the essay that had been published when I was in the 8th grade, I'd never written a word for anything, including the *Bloom Broadcaster*. I would keep that record intact during my two years at Northern Illinois, having little or no interest in working for the *Northern Star*. A wife and son have a tendency to limit your social activities. More importantly, I owed them whatever down time I had.

The one thing I can't remember is what exactly I wrote that caused Ms. Kohloff to ask me to stay after class for a second. I can't tell you if it was funny or profound or just the run-of-the-mill pap that she'd been seeing for decades.

Whatever it was, she asked me if I'd ever thought about writing for a living. I told her that I had not. "You should think about it," she said. "There's something there."

With those words, journalism officially became my fallback position. Did I actually believe I could make a living writing? I wasn't sure of that. But at least from then on I would tell my parents a happier story, that I had at last found my life's calling. Did I really believe it? Uh, no. How could I? I had not a shred of proof. But there just wasn't much else out there that I liked, so it was about time to set a goal.

When I think about it, I'm positive that I wasn't the only student that Mary Pierce made feel better about him or herself. Same for Vera Kohloff. My friend from Bloom, Larry McCoy, asked around about her and received this bit of feedback on Kohloff from a former student by the name of Trevor L. Davis: "This lady encouraged me to write with feeling and conviction," Davis wrote. "She was my World Literature teacher and an inspiration to me. She even sent an essay of mine about race and the civil rights movement down to the University of Illinois to a class of graduate students for a critique and feedback. She was stern but fair and she imparted her wisdom to her students in a way that left a lasting impression. If she were here today I would gladly thank her for giving me the skills that I used in both my professional and personal life. She was a great lady."

Yes, Trevor, she was.

AND THEN THERE were the notes and emails that flooded into the station for days and days on end.

I wish I had the time to individually thank each and every one of you who shared so much with me, just as I had shared so much with them over the course of 25 years.

Frankly, I was overwhelmed by the stories some of you told about the role that Boers and Bernstein had played in your life. I want you to know I read every one of those letters and I couldn't be happier that I did, even though many of them brought me to tears.

It's amazing what a little honesty can do. If there's one thing I learned over my 25 years in the business, it's that. I'd never been much of a sharer throughout my life, but that was yesterday and yesterday's gone.

I probably got around to answering about 300 or so of the emails, and if I didn't get to you, my deepest apologies. There were days in there when I just wasn't up to it, when my mouth was aching and the flesh just wasn't willing.

But that doesn't mean I don't deeply appreciate the time it took out of your life to write.

I've always been of the mind that my favorite guys in sports are the ones who get it, guys like Anthony Rizzo, Charles Tillman, and so many others who've made much of their life's work both during—and after—their careers about helping others.

In these turbulent times when we seem to be losing more and more of our humanity with each passing day, it's nice to know how many good, compassionate people are out there, sometimes losing sight amidst the terrorist attacks that plague our nation and so many others.

We might not have always been provided a warm sports' nest (there was some occasional yelling), but we did something for a whole lot of years that seemed to touch people from all walks of life.

That I was part of that will always be a source of endless pride. That so many people welcomed us into their cars, their homes, et al, will forever be seared in memory. I'm proud that so many said we made a difference in their lives, that the show brought special meaning to them in some of their darkest, most difficult days.

But going all the way back to guys like Patio Steve from Bolingbrook to Rafael from Berwyn to Irish Bill to Computer Boy Tom to NIU Dave to Cleveland Mike and so many others who there from the Pioneer days, there's no way to say thanks, especially for the first two who passed long ago.

That would include our friend Gary from Evanston, whose quirky personality and spot-on craps made him a Thursday star on Who Ya Crappin', especially the day he won our live competition.

But there were plenty other notables over the years: Dr. Dave, Mike from Milwaukee, who we finally got to see a picture of years after he started calling. Then there's Stan from Bellwood, Jock Itch Mitch (a helluva bowler), Frank from Oak Park, Bob in Niles/Park Ridge/places beyond, Northbrook Bob, Steph from Park Ridge, Tony from Matteson, Glenn from Downtown, Schmutzie, Mr. Mouth, and the ever-popular West Side Mike, who loved his hot garbage.

I'll stop there, noting there's a ton of names I missed, but you know who you are.

You're the ones who kept me going, who made me determined to get better at what I did, who enabled me to sit in that seat for the best 25 years of my life.

I wasn't sure what to make of any of it in 1992, when we were new and just trying to survive, hoping someday that the people

Loyal listeners and callers enabled me to spend the best 25 years of my life at The Score. *(Courtesy of 670 The Score)*

would just give us a chance—and you did exactly that, despite the awful signal and the other growing pains that the station has undergone over the years. I hope your patience was fully rewarded.

No matter if I was entertaining or boring, happy or sad, screaming at someone (maybe even you), we somehow managed to ride out the rough patches together.

I put this book together for those who cared, for those who shared with me both in emails and in person over the years of remotes and handshakes. I owed you at least that much.

We've shared a lot over the years, including perhaps the most awful day in our history on 9/11/01 and managed to come out on the other side, even though sports had a lot to do with the healing process our country needed after such unimaginable trauma.

But those days proved beyond a doubt what we were made of, how the human spirit isn't all that easy to conquer. I remember a lot of those conversations, a lot of sorrow, but always a ray of hope to go with it.

I mentioned during my final day on The Score that sitting there for as long as I did had been my honor. And no, I wasn't always proud of everything that happened in the 25 years. Sometimes I was too much of a jackoff even for my own good. And, yes, that happened more than once.

But I learned early on that no one is going to be perfect every day, every moment. Radio just isn't built that way. Hell, I feel lucky that I actually only had to be bleeped one time when I yelled, "Answer the fucking phone." I can't even remember why I did it, but I did.

I even did it without ever hating either of the Dans, McNeil or Bernstein. I like both of them. Hating one's radio partner seems to be quite the thing these days, even for shows that have been around forever.

It's also petty beyond belief. Now, I'm pretty sure I let pettiness get the best of me from time to time. But it isn't something you want to make a habit.

I'll leave with the two most underused words: Thank you. Oh, and here's two more: For everything. I still have some physical challenges in front of me, but I'll face them with the knowledge that I have a great family and way more friends than I would have ever imagined. No man should ask for more.

Epilogue

One more thing.

Because I was totally free for the first winter in my life, we decided to get out of the cold, snow, and ice of Chicago a few weeks after that final show, heading to Florida on Jan. 20 and not returning until April.

I thought of it as R & R, a chance to decompress and eventually collect enough thoughts in idle moments to write this book. And let me note here that I was the clubhouse leader in idle thoughts.

And, yes, I know the winter of 2016-17 wasn't fierce by Chicago standards, but I've become something I never thought possible—cold sensitive.

Losing damn near 50 pounds over the course of the two surgeries (I was at 177 in November) no doubt contributed, but even putting some of the weight back on didn't seem to help. After a lifetime of being about as immune to the cold as one can be, I was suddenly shivering at the mere thought of freezing temps.

So off we went.

The last great debate was deciding if I would treat myself to a retirement present, something I'd been mulling over for a while. And yes, I did have something in mind, something I'd been researching for months.

Thing is, one day I was all gung-ho, the next day I'd change my mind, deciding it would be far wiser not to spend any money.

I honestly didn't know what I was going to do. At least that's what I kept telling myself.

I had made an appointment from home with an auto dealership close to our house for the day after we arrived, but I didn't have to keep it. On the other hand, I'd given one of the salesmen specs for the exact car I wanted. He said he only had one available.

The suspense, if you want to think of it as such, didn't last long.

Even though I continued to ache and have days that were miserable, we were at the dealership the day after we got to Tampa. They had pulled the car right up front before we got there, noting that they couldn't find another one in the entire state of Florida.

I didn't believe that bullshit, but the car was gorgeous, although the mango color did take a little getting used to and sure seemed like a ticket magnet. Quick, somebody alert the Steger police.

About 10 minutes after the test drive we traded in our 2010 Chevy Equinox for—go ahead, take your best guess.

If you said a brand-new Dodge Charger, hit your ding button. This was the R/T Scatpack model with a little Super Bee featured in the front grill. It even has an electronic stop watch that will time you from zero to 60 and the quarter-mile if you so desire. No further comment on that is necessary.

So I have officially come full circle. It's perfect symmetry, at least in my mind. From one ill-fated Charger to one where I believe myself to be a much better driver.

And this one even has a shoulder harness that is quite comfortable and Carol even likes to drive it.

Will I eventually revert to my old form and drive like a deranged idiot?

Probably not, for two reasons. First, I left the car in Florida for now and the odometer was approaching 3,000 miles. But none of those came in quarter-mile increments like they did in the '60s. Second, this car isn't going anywhere.

I'm in this for the long haul, meaning the rest of my life. And I want my family to keep it. Forever.

Acknowledgments

To The Score's Mitch Rosen, who has been tireless in his efforts to help get this book off the ground, as have various members of the station's promotions department who dug up all kinds of goodies from over the years. I've had the great fortune to be associated with some of the best production people in business, all of whom contributed in a big way to the success of 25 years' worth of shows.

A lot of hard work goes into a successful career. No one can do it alone. This book was 25 years in the making—and I can guarantee you I would have never made it without so many people behind the scenes. I am forever in their debt. My eternal gratitude is to all of them.